The Green Guide to ENGLAND

The Green Guide to ENGLAND

John Button

Green Print
1989

Acknowledgements

All reference books rely heavily on other people's work and research, and this one is no exception. Thank you to all those who helped to collect the material for *The Green Guide to England*: the regional tourist board information officers, Graham Bell, Christine Brienne, David Button, Jon Carpenter, Margaret Elphinstone, Gillie Gould, Clare Hill, Sandy Irvine, Declan McHugh, Gerald Parsons, Marion Paul, Richard St George, Steve Skinner, Martin Stott, Ray Vail and Nancy Woodhead. And thanks to Eric Back for proofreading — again.

Copyright © John Button 1989

All rights reserved. No part of this publication may be reproduced, stored in a retrieval system, or transmitted, in any form or by any means, electronic, mechanical, photocopying, recording or otherwise, without the prior permission in writing of the publisher.

ISBN 1 85425 020 5

First published 1989 by Green Print
an imprint of The Merlin Press Ltd
10 Malden Road, London NW5 3HR (Tel: 01 267 3399)

Reprinted August 1989

Set in Palatino by the author and Saxon Printing Ltd
Printed in Great Britain by Biddles Ltd, Guildford

Contents

How to use this book	6
The green traveller	7
What England has to offer	13
The natural landscape	19
The peopled landscape	29
The growth of the Greens	38
Practical advice	47

The regions of England

Cumbria	63
Northumbria	69
North West	78
Yorkshire and Humberside	89
Heart of England	102
The Shires	112
East Anglia	122
West Country	135
Thames and Chiltern	151
South of England	161
South East	169
London	177

How to use this book

In many ways, *The Green Guide to England* is set out just like most other guidebooks. The difference is in its approach to the whole idea of tourism, and the things that it recommends you to do and look at while you are travelling.

The first chapter asks what travelling is all about, what we do it for, and what it does to the places we visit. The next three chapters look at what England has to offer to the visitor who travels with open eyes and an open mind. Then follows an introduction to the various aspects of the green movement in England, and a practical chapter dealing with things like food, money, travel and local contacts.

The heart of the book is the regional sections, where for convenience *The Green Guide* has divided the country up by regional tourist board areas: the maps at the section openings show which area is covered by each board. After a short introduction to the region, there is a description and directory for each of the major urban centres in that region, followed by a similar directory section for the region as a whole.

Although it is quite a task to fit the whole of England into one slim paperback volume, the aim has been to include as many worthwhile and visitable projects as possible under each heading, with enough information for you to be able to find them easily on the ground.

As always with books of this kind, we would appreciate feedback. If you come across inaccuracies, or new projects that you think should be included in future editions, please use the form at the end of the book to write to us.

The green traveller

I don't know about you, but though I usually enjoy visiting new and interesting places, I hate the thought of being seen as a tourist. I'll do almost anything to avoid the crowds at attractions and visitor centres, cringe at the overcommercialisation of our inheritance both natural and human, and detest the compulsory fun doled out for mass consumption.

'What a purist!' you might say; 'What's the harm in getting away from home and enjoying something a bit different for a change?' But travelling is a two-edged blade and can cut either way.

It cannot be denied that there are many wonderful and fascinating things in our world, and nothing can compare with the experience of seeing and feeling them at first hand. But in our quest for experience, often out of blind habit, we have virtually destroyed much of that very wonder and fascination, so we see only the ubiquitous postcard stand and souvenir stall wherever we go, and a car park fringed with litter.

When regular and long-distance travelling was reserved for the few who could afford it, and before the tourist industry was known as such, the enjoyment of new places was unimpeded by a mass of fellow-tourists, and the places which were visited were relatively unaffected by the people who came to experience them. Today things are very different. As John Julius Norwich writes at the

The green traveller

beginning of his travel anthology *A Taste for Travel*, 'The easier it becomes to travel, the harder it is to be a traveller.'

The average Briton in the late 1980s takes between two and three trips (involving nights away from home) a year within Britain, and nearly a third of us go abroad for a holiday. Those of us who stay in Britain are joined by thirteen million overseas visitors, a quarter of them from the USA and nearly half from our European neighbours. They spend almost five thousand million pounds in Britain, over a tenth of our foreign currency earnings, while we spend rather more than that on holidays abroad.

In addition to actual holidays, we will spend another eight or nine days on 'leisure day trips' — days at the beach, walking in the hills, visiting a stately home, or trying out the big dippers at Alton Towers.

Wherever you go in contemporary England, especially if you choose one of the more scenically attractive areas during the school summer holidays, you will find it hard to get away from the other people who are trying as hard as you are to get away from it all. Of course there *are* places that you will have to yourself, but they are not the places that appear in any tourist guide.

Several studies have shown that being a tourist is quite a stressful activity. For days at a time there is nowhere to relax properly. There are constant claims on your attention and on your purse, and traffic jams, heat and noise to contend with. You can't put your things anywhere and know they'll be safe, and you've no idea when you might encounter the next comfortable toilet.

Tourism is also stressful for the inhabitants and landscapes of the places being visited by large numbers of holiday-makers. It certainly brings much needed income into these areas, and the inhabitants of beautiful resorts do usually get some of the year to enjoy their surroundings without being trampled by visitors, yet tourists in bulk can completely destroy just those qualities of a place that they go there to enjoy.

The green traveller

You have to be something of a masochist to face one of the more popular West Country resorts on an average summer's day, but at least this is mostly human pressure upon the human-built environment, an environment which can usually take a good deal of wear and tear. Where masses of human feet leave tarmac and concrete surfaces and sally forth on to grassland or more fragile habitats, the results can be destructive in the extreme. Well-trodden paths, like those around Lulworth Cove in Dorset, parts of the Pennine Way, and the main pedestrian thoroughfares in the Lake District, need constant maintenance in order to prevent large-scale erosion. Unless imaginative provision is made for car parking, roadsides can become a mass of parked vehicles — the roads around Dartmeet in Devon and the approach to the Long Mynd from Church Stretton in Shropshire are but two such examples. While more immediately preventable, noise and litter both detract from the experience of being out in the countryside.

When pressure on tourist attractions mounts, it is very easy to see those who want to share the place with us as people who don't *really* appreciate where they are, people who are 'spoiling it for us'. Even those who stoutly defend their right to roam the English countryside can become quite fascist when talking about their fellow visitors.

Part of the answer, and one very consciously pursued by agencies like the Countryside Commission, has been to provide 'honeypots' for relatively passive visitors, leaving the remoter and more fragile places for the energetic seekers of space and freedom. Sometimes this means 'sacrificing' certain places, usually the more obvious attractions, in order to keep the hordes confined, but it also means that many unique and special places can only be experienced *en masse*.

Travelling may be an education, but tourism is most certainly an industry; like all industry, its primary purpose is to make money. Although many people involved in tourism see quality, fulfilment and standard of service as essential qualities of their work, financial considerations are inevitably paramount.

People who travel know this, and usually expect travelling to cost a lot of money; they even expect to be rooked fairly regularly. Those who live and work in beautiful places cannot be blamed for exploring ways of transferring urban wealth into their bank accounts, but there has to be a limit to what money can buy. There is a real danger of teaching our children — consciously or subconsciously — that what can be bought is more real than that which is available for the price of a little ingenuity and initiative. 'Wild and wonderful — £1 off,' reads a leaflet for a countryside attraction in Hampshire; 'a spectacular seashore world — two for the price of one' says an advert for a Devon marina.

The selling of our history in theme parks and heritage centres the length and breadth of the country may bring the past to life in a way that Victorian museums never did, but it also suggests (unless an enlightened local authority recognises that education is a right and not just a privilege) that excitement about and involvement with our heritage will inevitably cost — the phenomenon is so widespread that it has been dubbed 'the heritage industry'. Multinational companies, mindful of the direct links between their image and their profits, have stepped in to develop or sponsor such attractions, adding further to the commercialisation of tourism. No wonder the feeling is that when you are on the road, all that anyone wants is your money.

So how does the aware traveller do things any differently?

There are two questions which any green traveller must ask themself. The first is: 'Is my journey really necessary?' Many of us travel to get away from it all, often to the point where going away for our holidays has become something of a habit. Yet all the time 'there' becomes more and more like 'here', even down to the English Pub and the daily papers on the newsstands.

The green traveller

Maybe if we took more time and resources to make 'here' more like we envisage 'there' to be, 'here' would become more attractive. We would not only want to spend more time in our own neighbourhood, but would be able to spend more of our time enjoying beautiful surroundings.

The other important question, and a consideration central to green thinking, is: 'Am I respecting the landscape and culture of the place I am in?' Even in a small country like England there is an enormous variety of place and people, and the ecological maxim that diversity helps to create stability holds good in both environmental and cultural spheres. When so many economic and political pressures exist to bring about the uniformity which leads to profitable mass production and the boredom which leads to acquiescence, it is vital that we do everything in our power to maintain the unique character of local traditions and local landscapes.

What this means in practice is that the aware traveller will be something of a detective, taking notice of where they are, asking intelligent questions, supporting local initiatives, trying to understand rather than laying down the law. When they buy things to take home they will look for locally-made crafts, useful things that will not just gather dust until the next jumble sale. They will look for stimulation and clever ideas; real food, real ale and real people.

When it comes to their natural surroundings, the aware traveller knows that everywhere the environment is threatened by the activities of human beings, and that it isn't helped by the pressure of tourism. The Country Code is just a starting point: it's not just a matter of taking your litter home with you, for example, it's a matter of creating as little rubbish as possible in the first place. It isn't just a question of not trampling a farmer's crops or letting the livestock loose, it's respecting all living things and acknowledging that while you are sharing their territory you should be as careful as you would expect others to be when sharing yours.

The green traveller

The North American Sierra Club has a useful little reminder printed at the front of its wilderness guides: 'Take nothing but photographs,' it says, 'leave nothing but footprints.'

Having said all this, there is a terrible danger of holier-than-thouism creeping into our actions. Travelling in a more aware way makes the traveller no more virtuous, no better as a person, than any other. The simple truth is that travelling uses scarce resources however awarely it is done: all travellers are consumers, whether they are on the way to Leisureworld or an organic farm. If taken to its logical conclusion, a truly aware person probably wouldn't 'go on holiday' in the traditional sense at all — I doubt whether the native people of the Kalahari or the Amazon jungle would understand the concept.

Here then are some introductory thoughts for a guidebook with a difference, a guidebook which will help you to explore a country in which there are very many hopeful signs of an emerging future which seeks to enhance life — both human and non-human — rather than to destroy it.

Travelling in space is only one form of travelling, and perhaps what we need to do more than anything else is to integrate our experiences so that we do not constantly seek to find an escape. Once we can harness our imagination and arrange our surroundings as we want, travelling — through space, through time, through our lives — becomes an essential yet not overly important part of our experience. It becomes less and less important to get to places simply 'because they are there', but paradoxically we begin to gain more and more from our experience of where we are, wherever it happens to be. Then everywhere becomes important and everyone is a traveller. The Chinese sage Chuang Tzû left us with a nice conundrum when he wrote, three thousand years ago, that 'the good traveller knows not the destination, but the great traveller remembers not the starting point.'

Happy travels!

What England has to offer

Every traveller who knows anything at all about England will tell you that one of its most important qualities is its small scale: how on a walk of only two or three miles you can experience half a dozen different habitats, miniature landscapes and distant vistas, several different neighbourhoods and a variety of architectural styles. The essayist J.B. Priestley likened England to a box of tiny Japanese toys, each exquisite in its detail and each worthy of hours of detailed examination.

Thus the traveller who plans to see London in a day, or Dartmoor or the Lake District in a few hours, will be doing England an injustice. Whatever you do (and this applies equally to any of your travels), try not to bow to the temptation of rushing from one centre to another, imperilling wildlife, pedestrians, cyclists and your own health and sanity on the way. You will only find England when you get out of the car or the bus, and start exploring the side streets, the lanes and the footpaths.

England's variety starts deep down and long ago. As you will discover in the next chapter, few parts of the Earth's surface display such a wide variety of rocks and soil types as England's fifty thousand square miles (about a tenth of the area of the USA and a twentieth of that of the USSR).

What England has to offer

The adaptation of human life to the potential of the landscape has been equally various, and many English communities take pride in tracing hundreds of years of continuity in their local economies and customs. England is fortunate in never having been inundated (at least since Anglo-Saxon times) with an entirely alien culture; indeed, it is almost the only part of the globe to have been so fortunate. Until recently, that is.

From the end of the second world war, renewal and redevelopment have attacked England with a growing impact. Things were already so bad by the mid 1950s that architect Ian Nairn felt moved to coin the epithet 'subtopia' to describe the slab building, concrete expanses and boring 'landscaping' imported from downtown America.

The main aim of planners in the sixties, it seems, was to make everywhere look as much as possible like everywhere else. This was the time of the highrise, the city centre development, and the multistorey carpark. But it was also the period when national parks policy-makers started to use what teeth they had, and when urban conservation areas and areas of outstanding natural beauty started to mean anything.

A generation later, many of the mistakes of postwar policy are now coming home to roost. It has become increasingly obvious that a permissive approach will always favour the developer over the interests of community and conservation, and that however the sums are calculated, a financial equation which only takes immediate gains into account and ignores long-term costs is certain to prejudice both environmental and social wellbeing.

Thus alongside the rosy picture painted by the tourist brochures, the England of the nineties has inherited a chemical-intensive agriculture which threatens groundwater supplies, coal-fired power stations which spew pollution far across the North Sea, thirty-year old nuclear power stations which nobody knows how to dismantle, a struggling public transport system, highrise estates

What England has to offer

marked by poverty, deprivation and graffiti, and a legacy of dereliction following the decline of traditional heavy industries.

Most travel guides will tell you nothing of this, because environmental degradation is not a great tourist attraction. They want to show you only pretty villages, craggy mountains, parks and museums, golden sands and stately homes. The truth is that England is both, and the intelligent traveller will want to know about both.

The coexistence of the two Englands (and many people are worried about the growing divide) is important for another reason. Some of the initiatives described in the *Green Guide* are taking place in the traditionally 'beautiful' parts of England, but many are happening in just those places where ten years ago the outlook seemed the worst. Money has always been able to buy certain varieties of prettiness, splendour and charm, but only recently have relatively poor communities acquired the resources to create an environment of their own which they can be proud of.

Whatever else money can buy, it cannot buy community, and groups of people throughout the country, recognising this, have started to become involved in grassroots initiatives to improve their surroundings and their communities. In many ways and for a variety of reasons, England is experiencing now many of the problems that other parts of the western world will face in the near future, and this is one way in which the enquiring traveller from overseas can learn a great deal.

If this description of what England has to offer has been less than appetising, it is only because the aware traveller knows when the conventional guides are telling half-truths, and it is unnecessary to paint a picture only in pastel shades in order to attract folk to our shores. You can obtain reams of tourist literature free from any information office; if the *Green Guide* simply repeated verbatim what was offered there it would be poor value indeed.

So how do you make contact with England as it really

What England has to offer

is? If only there were an easy way! If you live in Britain and maintain a healthy interest in current affairs, then it is probably best just to keep your ears and eyes open as you travel.

Libraries and tourist information centres are obvious points of call for both domestic and foreign travellers, and twenty minutes' browse will usually provide a sheaf of interesting reading matter.

Wherever you are in England you will not be far from a public library, and nearly all have a collection of local material and a noticeboard with details of local events and places to visit. If you are staying in the same place for a few days you may be able to borrow books.

The English Tourist Board (Thames Tower, Black's Road, Hammersmith, London W6 9EL; Tel: 01-846 9000) is the statutory body promoting tourism in England. They can provide general information, and there are departments which deal specifically with foreign visitors with particular interests, and with research enquiries. Preliminary enquiries from overseas can usually be dealt with by British Tourist Authority offices in your own country — there are offices in 21 countries, including four in the USA (Chicago, Dallas, Los Angeles and New York). Tourism in England is administered by twelve regional tourist boards; these are the best places from which to request more detailed information, and many cities, towns and districts produce their own literature. One useful free booklet produced by the BTA is a complete list of tourist information centres in Britain. The addresses of each of the twelve regional boards will be found in the appropriate regional sections later in the book.

While there is a superabundance of guidebooks to England and its constituent parts, there are very few books which give an overall impression of what England is actually like; this could be because it is so hard to encapsulate the variety of the country between two covers.

Of the many single-volume guides to England you could buy there isn't one that I can recommend wholeheartedly, and most are so hefty that you need to think several times before deciding to lug it around the country. The annual *Let's Go* budget guide to Britain

What England has to offer

and Ireland, put together by Harvard students and distributed in England by Pan Books, is probably the best buy, though a good up-to-date map is all you really need (see page 57). If you want an overview before you start travelling, among the best of the comprehensive handbooks to England is *The Shell Guide to England*, edited by John Hadfield. Then there are the more individual and sometimes idiosyncratic accounts by a single author, like John Hillaby's *Journey Through Britain*, the historian W.G. Hoskins' *One Man's England*, the artist David Gentleman's beautifully illustrated books, and the activist Bea Campbell's *Wigan Pier Revisited*. For a more in-depth view of urban Britain try Paul Harrison's *Inside the Inner City*, or Geoffrey Beattie's books, *Survivors of Steel City* and *Making It*. For the rural scene read Marion Shoard's *This Land is Our Land* and Howard Newby's *The Countryside in Question*.

The rest of this chapter is written primarily for overseas visitors — it attempts to answer three of the big questions that anyone planning a holiday in England will ask first:
— Where should I go?
— When should I go?
— How much detailed arranging should I do in advance?

Having said earlier that it is counterproductive to try to see too much of England in one trip, where you decide to go will depend very much on your interests, where you have been before, and where your friends live.

Authors of guidebooks inevitably give prominence to their own favourite places, and I shall not hesitate to tell you mine! If I were visiting England for the first time and had a couple of weeks in which to see a good cross section of the country, I think my list of cities would include London (three or four days, at the *end* of my visit), Bristol, Liverpool, Sheffield and York. I would want three or four days walking through a varied rural landscape — Dorset, perhaps, or the hills of Shropshire, or the North Yorkshire Coast Path, and I would arrange to visit half a dozen places which particularly interested me — a communal group, perhaps; an organic farm; a craft workshop. I might well join a course or a workshop for two or three days during my stay, both to learn new skills and to meet

What England has to offer

people in more than the superficial way that travelling usually permits. What I would try very hard to avoid is the tourist traps at peak times, though the sorts of places that a green traveller will find will not usually be unbearable even at the height of summer.

Compared with many parts of the world, England is an interesting and comfortable place to visit at any time of the year. It has a notoriously fickle climate (not helped by its population's rather negative preoccupation with the weather), and a visit between December and March may mean delays and slight inconveniences, but a sunny spell in October can be far more conducive to a pleasant stay than a dull week in June. If you want to avoid the height of the summer season try not to visit during the school holidays, which are fairly uniform throughout England (usually late July to early September).

Many travellers limit themselves by planning too much in advance. What I like to do when travelling in a country that I don't know well is to plan the trip only in broad outline, leaving space to follow up kind invitations and fascinating sidetracks. Even in July and August it will nearly always be easy to find somewhere to stay in most parts of England. It is well worth writing or telephoning ahead to plan those parts of your visit that you know you want to do, but leaving spaces allows for the serendipity of the new friend who insists on showing you the stone circles of Dartmoor or the windmills of Norfolk, or for following up that interesting article on city farms in London's Dockland.

The natural landscape

While the English may not always appreciate or look after their natural environment, most would readily agree that the English landscape is both precious and unique. 'Land is life,' wrote conservationist Herbert Girardet in 1976. 'Land is constant while human life is transient upon it, and it is the duty of every generation to leave the land at least as vigorous and fertile as they found it.'

Yet there has probably never been another culture or another area where there is so little awareness of what land is, and of its crucial role in ecological wellbeing. Since 1950 England has lost a third of its heaths and upland grasslands; half of its ancient woodlands, limestone pavements and lowland marshes; four-fifths of its chalk and limestone grasslands; and over 95% of its lowland herb-rich grassland.

Fewer than 2% of England's population work on the land, and four out of five live in a city or town. Even most of those who live in the country depend on nearby urban centres for employment and services — one of the few ways of making a living in today's English countryside is from travellers like you! Because the English have so few links with the land under their feet, they often have very little idea of what harm is being done to it in the name of progress.

Most parts of England have been inhabited by human beings almost continuously for two thousand years or

The natural landscape

more. The English concept of 'wilderness', therefore, tends to be an overgrown path down the side of the house rather than a wolf-inhabited forest three days' march from the nearest human habitation. The 'natural environment' sought out by holiday-makers is far from what nature would create if left to its own devices, being in reality the result of centuries of complex interaction between nature and human influence.

Yet there are still many relatively wild corners of England, and many more that are being carefully managed to ensure that no unnecessary harm is done to them. The growing awareness that has led to an understanding for the need for conservation comes largely from a particularly English 'scientific' fascination with the details of the natural world. Whether in geology or botany, ornithology or meteorology, the early impetus for a detailed understanding of nature came largely from English amateurs and, like them, the discerning traveller will usually want to know and understand some of the ecological complexities of the places they visit during their travels.

Geology

Nowhere else in the world has such a variety of rocks, minerals and landforms within such a small area as does England, though you will need to travel north and west into Scotland and Wales to find Britain's oldest geological formations.

England's oldest rocks are to be found in the Pennines and in the highland areas of Devon and Cornwall; in general the underlying formations become more and more recent as you travel south-eastwards. On a journey from Sheffield to London you will cross Carboniferous coal measures, the sandstones of the Trent valley, the limestones of the Leicestershire hills, the valley clays of Northamptonshire, the Chiltern Hills with their fossil-filled chalk, and the deep heavy muds of the London basin — all this within 150 miles.

The natural landscape

If you are fascinated by things geological, then any holiday in England should include a visit to the Geological Museum in London's South Kensington. As well as housing one of the most complete mineral collections and geological libraries in the world, the Museum shop also stocks a wide range of literature about the geology of England, including all the published sheets of the Geological Survey. These are available for most of England at two scales: 1/250,000 and 1/50,000. The larger-scale maps are sometimes available in two versions, one showing the underlying rock formations ('solid'), the other showing what is to be found at the land surface ('drift'); in less geologically complex areas both are shown on the same sheet.

Landforms

Geomorphology is the study of different landforms and how they have come to be the way they are. Again, for such a small area England has an enormous variety of landforms, from the drowned river valleys (rias) of Cornwall and Devon to the chalk cliffs of Kent; the swallowholes and subterranean rivers of the Yorkshire Dales to the hanging valleys and knife-edge ridges of the Lake District.

Geomorphology is a fairly new field of study, and certainly a very recent newcomer to the literature designed for an interested lay readership. Andrew Goudie and Rita Gardner are currently the most fluent describers of England's landforms. Their *Discovering Landscape in England and Wales* (Unwin Hyman, 1985, £14.95) gives more than fifty well-illustrated examples of regional landforms, while the more recent and more popular *Landshapes* (written with Denys Brunsden and David Jones, David and Charles, 1988, £14.95) gives a more general overview of the variety of the country's physical landscape.

Rivers and seas

England's rivers and streams, unlike those of colder climes which regularly freeze in winter or those of the tropics that vanish entirely during the dry season, are a comforting and consistent focal point of the English landscape. Standing on an old humpback bridge

The natural landscape

watching the endless flow of water — or better still finding the perfect bank for dangling your travel-weary feet in it — is an ideal way of relaxing both mind and body.

But England's rivers are under dire threat. In many areas of heavy industry the desire to dangle feet in the water disappeared more than a century ago, but most of the rivers of rural England, or at least those that pass through intensively-farmed areas, are now so heavily polluted with nitrates, pesticides and farm effluent that bathing is a considerable health hazard.

Detailed, yet very readable, information about the current state of water quality in England's rivers is included in an excellent collection of essays, edited by Edward Goldsmith and Nicholas Hildyard, called *Green Britain or Industrial Wasteland?* (Polity, 1986, £4.95). The beauty and variety of the country's rivers are captured in *Rivers of Britain* by Richard and Nina Muir (Michael Joseph, 1986, £14.95), which includes many striking photographs.

When it comes to England's coastlines, a major tourist attraction, the story is, if anything, even worse. Far from being the silver sea in which an emerald isle is set, England's coastal waters are too often used as an all-purpose tip with very little regard to wildlife or bathers alike. Arsenic in the Humber, ammonium sulphate off Teesside, heavy metals in the Mersey, sewage sludge in the Thames, nitrates off East Anglia — these are only some of the hazards noted in a recent Greenpeace survey.

England's coastline may be beautiful to look at, but the entire high water line is strewn with seaborne rubbish, and at many of the most famous seaside resorts — Weston-super-Mare, Eastbourne and Yarmouth among them — swimmers may find themselves sharing the sea with human excrement and multicoloured toilet paper.

Greenpeace's beautifully illustrated book, *Coastline* (Kingfisher, 1987, £14.95), chronicles both scenic highlights and environmental threats around the country's 1,400 mile seaboard, while detailed information about the relative cleanliness of England's beaches is contained in the Marine Conservation Society's *Good Beach Guide* (Ebury, 1988, £5.95). If you plan to spend some of your holiday

The natural landscape

swimming and sunbathing, or undertaking one of the long-distance coastal walks, you may be very glad that you have checked your selected beaches in this handy volume.

Natural history

The rich variety of the English landscape provides the setting for a unique and fascinating range of plants and animals, yet, because England is a small country densely populated by human beings, pressure on natural habitats is often extreme and ecologically disastrous. The very species that naturalists and the interested public travel many miles to visit can become the victims of their own popularised rarity, and protected sites are often so small that any change in the surrounding area can have tragic results.

The most important advice to any green traveller where wildlife is concerned is to make your presence in fragile habitats as light and as short as possible. The ecological web is a complex one, of which you are a part just as much as the rest of the natural history of the place you are in.

Many visitors to nature reserves and other relatively wild areas know instinctively that the wild inhabitants of these places should be respected; others want to know about those inhabitants and their complex interactions in more detail. Ecological understanding is the key to such wisdom, and in England there is a long tradition of exploring the details of the country's natural history. For many years, sadly, it was generally understood that this meant hunting out as many different species as possible, killing them, and mounting them in glass cases for other collectors to admire. Although collectors are still responsible for the destruction of many rare specimens, and the debate between conservationists and men with guns goes on, there are today literally thousands of amateur naturalists patiently observing and recording their local wildlife from a non-threatening distance, building up a more detailed picture of the country's non-human population than ever before.

The natural landscape

Many parts of England are now covered by detailed nature guides, often written or sponsored by the local Trust for Nature Conservation. The Royal Society for Nature Conservation (The Green, Nettleham, Lincoln LN2 2NR) will be able to provide details for specific areas that you plan to visit, while an sae to the Natural History Book Service (2 Wills Road, Totnes, Devon TQ9 5XN) will bring you a free up-to-date list of almost every book currently in print pertaining to wildlife and countryside, both of England and beyond.

'Complete Guides' to England's wildlife are virtually guaranteed to be fairly superficial, but of the several available, Michael Chinery's *Field Guide to the Wildlife of Britain and Europe* (Kingfisher, 1987, £6.95) is not bad; it doesn't cover plants, so you'll need a good flower book too (see below).

Trees and woodland

Trees are an essential part of the English landscape, adding immeasurably to the almost universal verdure commented on by visitors from more extreme climes. Yet England has retained less of its native woodland than any country in Europe, which is a very good reason for conserving as much as possible of what has survived. Sherwood Forest in Nottinghamshire and the New Forest in Hampshire are mere shadows of their former selves, while the mighty and ancient Forest of Arden has left little trace on the Warwickshire landscape.

To add to the loss of 50% of England's old deciduous forest and more than a quarter of its hedgerow trees in the last 35 years, Dutch Elm Disease has claimed 15 million trees, and the great storm of October 1987 another 15 million in South-East England.

Having done its best in its first decades of existence to regiment upland valleys with boring conifer stands, the Forestry Commission has recently begun to recognise that the discerning traveller appreciates well-planned forestry, and that tourism can be encouraged by the provision of walks through varied forest habitats, information services, and volunteer conservation projects.

The affinity between people and trees has been

The natural landscape

demonstrated by tree-hugging campaigns from India to Sweden; a recent campaign to save two ancient oak trees in a Wiltshire market town elicited nationwide concern and concerted media coverage. In this case the developer still won the case and the trees fell, but the tide of interest is turning.

The Forestry Commission (231 Corstorphine Road, Edinburgh EH12 7AT) produces two excellent booklets about the tree species you will find in England; called *Conifers* and *Broadleaves*, each costs 25p. The Ordnance Survey and publishers Michael Joseph have collaborated to produce a very good series of *Woodland Walk Guides*; five volumes at £5.95 each cover England, and each volume includes detailed maps and ecological information. The Woodland Trust (Autumn Park, Dysart Road, Grantham, Lincolnshire NG31 6LL) owns and manages woodlands throughout the country, and part of their policy is to encourage public access; they can provide a list of woodlands in their trust.

Wildflowers

Buttercup-yellow meadows and bluebell woods feature in almost every tourist brochure about England, but the truth is that in many places the country's flora is threatened. If you know where to look you will still find herb-rich meadows, anemone-strewn woodland glades, and the rare plant communities of unimproved uplands and marshes, but you must be very careful not to disturb them. Some people inexplicably continue to pick rare flowers, even to take whole plants, ignoring that plant's right to survive even though it can't run away and hide.

Alastair Fitter's *New Generation Guide to Wild Flowers* (Collins, 1987, £6.95) is the best of the portable guides, though the Reader's Digest hardback *Field Guide to the Wild Flowers of Britain* (1983, £8.95) is hard to beat for design and user-friendliness. A beautifully written and hauntingly illustrated introduction to the flora of the British islands is provided by Richard Mabey and Tony Evans in *The Flowering of Britain* (Arrow, 1982, £7.95). Information about endangered species, together with an illustrated leaflet about protected species, can be obtained from the Fauna and Flora Preservation Society, London Zoo, Regents Park, London NW1 4RY.

The natural landscape

Birds

Birdwatching attracts more interest from wildlife amateurs in England than any other subject, and well it might. The country's favoured island position at the crossroads of migration routes, together with its rich variety of habitats, provides ornithologists with a bounty of avian riches.

If one particular aspect of this bounty had to be chosen for special mention, it might be the coastal wetlands of North Norfolk or the Severn Estuary, where the Wildfowl Trust's renowned Slimbridge Sanctuary sometimes provides a temporary home for 20,000 ducks and swans, not to mention the many thousands of migrant waders. On the other hand, the cliffs of the South-West provide the ideal habitat for great colonies of seabirds, while even in urban areas the variety of bird life is considerable.

Yet at least three dozen bird species have shown an appreciable long-term decline in recent years, including such favourites as the nightingale, the heron and the kingfisher, all dependent on a narrow range of habitat. Pollution and habitat loss are the main problems, though birdwatchers must always take care to make their presence as little felt as possible.

The best guide to the birds you might see in England is *The Shell Guide to the Birds of Britain and Ireland* (Michael Joseph, 1983, £8.95), which shows birds in flight and in seasonal plumage as well as in the conventional standing poses. The Royal Society for the Protection of Birds (The Lodge, Sandy, Bedfordshire SG19 2DL) is the country's premier ornithological association; membership entitles you to free access to their 121 reserves throughout Britain.

Nature conservation

There is a long history of local conservation initiatives in England, and for its size the country has the largest membership of voluntary conservation bodies of any in the world. The other side of the conservation coin is that less government money is spent on protecting wildlife

The natural landscape

and habitats than almost anywhere in the western world — less is spent on the country's national parks each year by central government (around £10 million) than is spent subsidising London's Royal Opera House.

England has seven national parks, designated between 1951 and 1955, which cover nearly a tenth of the land area. Many imaginative schemes for the management of landscape and local inititiative have been introduced in recent years, some of which are described in the regional sections later in the *Guide*. There has even been some limited attempt to introduce agricultural and forestry policies which are appropriate to the ecologies of particular areas, though it is dispiriting to see the many scars that have been made on some of the country's finest landscapes in the name of economic progress.

If strict guidelines cannot be laid down for the national parks, inappropriate development is even more threatening in the country's 31 Areas of Outstanding Natural Beauty and along the 500-odd miles of Heritage Coast. The English are experts at designating areas and writing reports about them, but when it comes to implementation the wheels turn excruciatingly slowly. Many of the problems are to do with the peculiarly English approach to land ownership. Unlike many other countries, a minute proportion of designated conservation areas is in public ownership. Many landowners do take their responsibilities seriously, but many more either will not, or cannot afford to.

At the smaller scale of the fifteen hundred or so nature reserves, the situation is in general much better, since a large proportion are either owned or managed by responsible conservation bodies. On the other hand, small nature reserves are constantly threatened by changes taking place beyond their boundaries, and because conservation is the primary aim, public access often has to be strictly limited.

In an important 1984 report the Nature Conservancy Council described the country as a land in crisis, suffering

The natural landscape

'alarming losses in national natural heritage'; they called the resources available for conservation 'derisory', land-use policies 'unsympathetic' and the legal framework 'inadequate'. And that was an official report.

If you are interested in nature conservation and plan to spend any length of time in one area, it is well worth getting in touch with the local county trust for nature conservation: the local trusts are listed under 'wildlife' in each regional section. The Royal Society for Nature Conservation (The Green, Nettleham, Lincoln LN2 2NR) is the umbrella organisation for all of the county trusts.

For an overview of nature conservation in England, read the Nature Conservancy Council's report *Nature Conservation in Great Britain*, from which the above quotations are taken (£7.50 from the NCC, Northminster House, Peterborough PE1 1UA; a summary is also available for £1.25). The full and often depressing story of the national parks is told in Ann and Malcolm MacEwen's *Greenprints for the Countryside* (Allen and Unwin, 1987, £8.95), while *Countryside Conflicts* by Philip Lowe and friends (Temple Smith, 1986, £8.95) includes an excellent history of the British conservation movement. *The Macmillan Guide to Britain's Nature Reserves* (1986, £12.95) is a beautifully illustrated and detailed guide to 2,000 reserves all over Britain — a thick volume to be consulted in a library rather than lugged around.

The Countryside Commission (John Dower House, Crescent Place, Cheltenham GL50 3RA) is an excellent source for material about countryside conservation in England, and much of their literature is free. One very useful publication is a map called *Protected Areas in the United Kingdom*; if you slip this into your pack you can be sure not to miss any important wildlife highlights.

The foremost voluntary countryside organisation in England is the Council for the Protection of Rural England (4 Hobart Place, London SW1W 0HY), which campaigns on a wide range of issues from pollution control to rights of way. There are CPRE groups in every county of England, and the main office will be able to give you addresses.

The peopled landscape

There are very few places in England which have been entirely untouched by people. The hills of Devon and Cornwall, the moorlands of Yorkshire and the mountains of Cumbria once maintained human communities far larger than they now support, and even landscapes which appear to be the epitome of natural grandeur show many signs of human involvement when examined more closely.

On the other hand, there are many parts of England where you have to look quite closely to see the signs of nature's involvement in the environment, and a degree of urbanisation has been part of the English scene from Roman times onwards. Buildings (or at least the remains of them) from every period of England's history have been carefully preserved against the ravages of time and developers: many an American tourist comments on just how much history you can still see in Olde Englande.

A great deal of England's built heritage has been neatened and beautified for the interested visitor and sightseer; buildings are, after all, the fabric and framework of the 'heritage industry'. A great many more of the country's interesting and useful old buildings are still decaying and threatened by the bulldozer, especially the smaller and less obviously attractive houses, and many Victorian mills and factories not now needed for their original purpose.

The peopled landscape

Few countries have such a compulsive interest in local history as does England, and it usually takes little effort to find somebody willing to tell you about the Iron Age fort on Windmill Hill or the last train that ran to Little Piddlington. It helps a great deal, though, if you have a modicum of prior knowledge and understanding, and are genuinely interested in what the churchwarden has to tell you about the rood screen in the chancel and the gravestone of Shakespeare's Dark Lady (or was she a White Lady?) in the crypt.

Prehistory

Because England has been so densely settled for so long, the landscape is thick with reminders from the period before written records can tell us about the land and its inhabitants. You can visit massive hillforts like Maiden Castle in Dorset or Danebury in Hampshire, or the burial mounds ('barrows') at Stoney Littleton near Bath or Pimperne in Dorset, while many people's first visit to England would be incomplete without seeing the three-thousand-year-old temple at Stonehenge.

These are only the highlights, however, and there are many other things to see. If you know what you are looking for, you will soon be able to discern the telltale ramparts of Iron Age forts on almost every prominent hill and headland; the circles of neolithic houses on the moors of Yorkshire; the lines of ancient trackways.

A good general introduction to English prehistory is Edward Dyer's *Guide to Prehistoric England* (Penguin, 1980, £4.95), while Richard Muir's *Countryside Encyclopaedia* (Macmillan, 1988, £14.95) provides good entries on specific topics, with hints for further reading.

Local museums are a good source of archaeological information, and are usually delighted to answer specific queries. Many ancient monuments in England are looked after by English Heritage (15-17 Great Marlborough Street, London W1V 1AF); membership brings you a useful countrywide guide and free entrance to all their properties, though many of the more isolated and less-visited sites are free anyway.

If local legend and mystery are your cup of tea, you can carry with you either Jennifer Westwood's fascinating and well-researched *Albion: A Guide to Legendary Britain* (Paladin, 1987, £6.95), or Guy Williams' *Guide to the Magical Places of England, Wales and Scotland* (Constable, 1987, £7.95), chock full of headless horsemen, ghostly figures and fiery dragons.

History

How to do justice to English history in a couple of paragraphs? It is of course impossible, but the aware traveller will inevitably want to know at least a little about how places and people have come to be how they are, and will want some kind of historical framework into which to fit new sights and information.

To a certain extent, the experience of old things is a physical and emotional one; you will always find tourists wandering round a medieval abbey who hardly look up from the guidebook; however much they know, they will hardly have seen the place. Yet there are far more who 'do' the same abbey in ten minutes, pausing longer at the postcard rack than at the richly-carved romanesque archway through which generations of teachers and healers have passed.

You can read about the past, but it is also important to experience what remains of the past, whether it be the memories of older people or memories locked into the landscape. As the green philosopher Murray Bookchin explains, 'We are the heirs of a history that can teach us what we must avoid if we are to escape immolation and what we must pursue if we are to realise freedom and self-fulfilment.'

Yet this heritage too, just like England's natural heritage, is at risk. It is at risk from those who believe that anything old is useless, and from those who believe that 'heritage' is simply another way of making money. The value of historical insight is in understanding both past and present, acknowledging that we too shall soon be history. What will future generations remember *us* by?

The peopled landscape

A well-written single-volume history of England which incorporates radical new insights is long overdue, though G.M. Trevelyan's well-tested *English Social History* (Penguin, 1963, £4.95) is a good start. W.G. Hoskins' *The Making of the English Landscape* (Penguin, 1969, £4.95) is an excellent introduction to English local history, beautifully written.

English Heritage (see under 'prehistory') looks after many important historic buildings in England; a further two hundred or so are owned and maintained by The National Trust, which also protects nearly 500 miles of coastline and a million acres of wildest Britain. Membership of the Trust (36 Queen Anne's Gate, London SW1H 9AS) brings you their annual handbook, which is full of very useful information for travellers, and lets you into most of their properties without further payment.

As with prehistory, museums are a very good source of local information, and almost every public library has a section of books of local interest which you can consult.

Agriculture and countryside

It is only relatively recently that the English left the land. A hundred and fifty years ago there were few people who were not also landworkers; even forty years ago there were four times as many farmworkers as there are today. The link with the soil is for many people through their garden, and the English are renowned gardeners. But most food now comes from labour and energy intensive agriculture, a system which is, quite simply, unsustainable. It depends on fertilisers and pesticides, endless supplies of oil, and subsidies which favour a few millionaire farmers while many small and part-time farmers face bankruptcy.

The trend towards large-scale intensive farming has inevitably left its marks on the English landscape, from the barley prairies of Lincolnshire to the massive dairy farms of the West Country. England has lost a quarter of its hedgerows since 1948, and nitrate pollution from fertilisers endangers the drinking water supply of many parts of lowland England. It would be too easy to blame only the farmers for the damage; economics and official policy have much to answer for. The fact remains, however, that current ways of doing things are leading to ecological and social bankruptcy.

With few exceptions, rural England is but a pale shadow of its former self. The English village, its school and post office closed and properties bought as commuting bases and second homes, is often dying or dead. Because there is no work, no entertainment, no public transport and nowhere they can afford to live, the young people have moved out. Agricultural workers are still poorly paid and poorly housed, while the most profitable farms are bought up by insurance companies and food chains. Yes, it is depressing to know that many of the pretty villages and farms you see on your travels are, as Howard Newby has put it, 'sanitized versions of Olde Worlde Englande completely divorced from the reality of rural life'.

There are a few cheering exceptions, like the villages of Ardington in Oxfordshire and Monyash in Derbyshire, or the other initiatives mentioned in the regional sections later in the *Guide*, but communities and landscapes only thrive if they are alive and healthy. Too many aspects of rural England have been frozen in aspic for the passive amusement of wealthy incomers and undiscriminating tourists.

Of a number of recent books on agriculture and rural change in England, three which stand out are Oliver Rackham's excellent *The History of the Countryside* (Dent, 1987, £8.95); Howard Newby's incisive *The Countryside in Question* (Century, 1988, £7.95); and the same author's hard-hitting *Green and Pleasant Land? Social Change in Rural England* (Wildwood House, 1985, £5.95), which tells what life is really like for those who live and work in England's countryside.

The built environment

Steel, concrete and glass may be the prevalent building materials in the England of the late twentieth century, just as they are in almost every corner of the globe, but this is a recent innovation. Patterns of traditional English

The peopled landscape

building are closely related to the materials which were easily available; thus the ubiquitous yellow brick of the London region gives way to the grey stone of Oxfordshire or the flint of East Anglia. Further afield, golden Bath stone, the red sandstone of the West Midlands, or the granite and slate of the Lake District proclaim a local identity which is essential for residents and visitors alike. Who wants to live in — or visit — a place that looks just like every other?

Thanks largely to the efforts of conservationists, you can still see churches and castles, manor houses and cottages, mills and markets, dating from almost every period of English architecture. Many of the best are open to the public, since today this is one of the few ways of providing the resources for their upkeep. Many more, running into the hundreds of thousands, are at least nominally protected by 'listed building' legislation, and it is this extensive body of building that gives the English landscape much of its character.

Though there is more awareness of the intrinsic value of old buildings than there was twenty years ago, and though it has been shown time and again that renovation is cheaper and gives better results than rebuilding, much of the country's built heritage is still under threat. Old buildings are not only attractive; with imaginative planning they can be used, not just as houses and offices, but as centres for the community's social and economic activities. Putting the contents of a stately home behind barriers for a stream of tourists to gawp at from a distance may pay the bills, but turning the stables into craft workshops and the ballroom into a community arts space will do a lot more for the local population, attract more discerning visitors, *and* pay the bills.

Alec Clifton-Taylor's *The Pattern of English Building* (Faber, 1987, £14.95) is a classic, with many beautiful illustrations, while R.W. Brunskill's *Illustrated Handbook of Vernacular Architecture* (Faber, 1987, £7.50) is an excellent introduction to building styles, materials and house construction. If you enjoy wandering round cities looking at the buildings, Lewis Braithwaite's *Exploring British Cities* (Black, 1986, £9.95) is a detailed guide, illustrated with fascinating extracts from Victorian Ordnance Survey maps. Nikolaus Pevsner's outstanding achievement in chronicling every almost every historically important building in the country can be found in the relevant county volumes of *The Buildings of England*, which you can consult in local libraries.

The National Trust (see under 'history') maintains many historic buildings, from 'stately homes' and manor houses to farmhouses and dovecotes. English Heritage (see under 'prehistory') looks after a number of older buildings. If the built environment is of particular interest to you, the Civic Trust (17 Carlton House Terrace, London SW1Y 5AW) is the country's foremost urban conservation organisation and will answer specific questions.

The industrial landscape

England, with its growing overseas empire and scientific discoveries, was at the turn of the nineteenth century the birthplace of modern industrialism. While industry supposedly 'made Britain great', it also caused a great deal of misery and environmental damage — by 1840 the average life expectancy of a Manchester labourer was 17. The social divide between the labouring poor and the landed rich (a Rutland landowner in the same year could expect to live to 52 years of age) has been a mark of English society to the present day, explaining to a large extent the narrowing yet very clear cultural chasm which still exists between the largely Labour-voting poor and the mainly Conservative-voting rich.

The early expansion of industry has in many places also led to its early demise, with England being rapidly overhauled in the high stakes of industrial competition by the newly-mechanised nations like West Germany and Japan. This has led to the wholesale closing of cotton and steel mills, mines and railways, leaving scars both on the communities established to operate them and the landscapes disfigured by their waste products.

Today's pattern of work in England owes much — both good and not so good — to working traditions which are many decades old. There are crafts like metal toolmaking

The peopled landscape

and superb glassmaking in which England still leads the field; yet many opportunities for making work more useful and fulfilling are lost, often because people are unable or unwilling to try radically different alternatives. Many of those alternatives — flexible trade unionism, co-operatives, credit unions, community businesses, socially useful work — are English inventions, and you can read about some of them later in the *Guide*. There is still an enormous reluctance to experiment, however, leaving communities without any apparent purpose, and refusing to acknowledge the acute environmental problems caused by unaware industrial development.

For an understanding of the social aspects of industrialism in England, the classic (if a little dated) is E.P. Thompson's *The Making of the English Working Class* (Penguin, 1967, £5.95), while a green perspective on current dilemmas facing industry and industrialism is provided by James Robertson in *Future Work* (Temple Smith, 1985, £6.95). The gruesome details of the pollution caused by industry will be found in Edward Goldsmith and Nicholas Hildyard's *Green Britain or Industrial Wasteland?* (Polity, 1986, £4.95). On a more positive note, the semi-official body that looks after the interests of small craft industries in England, COSIRA (Council for Small Industries in Rural Areas, 141 Castle Street, Salisbury SP1 3TP) publishes a useful guide called *Craft Workshops in the English Countryside* (AA, 1987, £3.95). More details of green economic initiatives are given in the next chapter.

The industrial revolution of the nineteenth century was based on the availability of cheap and easily-harnessed power supplies, and the energy supply industry, based first on water, then on coal, and now also on oil and nuclear power, has continued to have a profound effect both on England's economy and ecology. If you travel in Yorkshire or the West Midlands, you cannot avoid seeing the scars of the coal industry; were Three Mile Island or Chernobyl to happen in England you would be allowed nowhere near the scars for many decades, and in such a small and densely-populated country, a nuclear accident could put a large proportion of it out of bounds.

Another aspect of the English landscape to which

The peopled landscape

attention will not normally be drawn by your travel agent is its use by the military. Nearly half a million acres of England are owned by the Ministry of Defence, including large tracts of land in all but one (Exmoor) of the country's national parks. With few exceptions this land is closed to the public, so you will probably not notice the military presence. The low-flying jets whistling down the valleys of the Lake District cannot, however, fail to affect you if you venture on the fells. Additional to MoD-owned land in England are the hundred-odd US bases, conveniently located away from North America on what has been called 'an unsinkable aircraft carrier'. All this and more awaits the attention of the aware traveller in England.

The Energy Fix by Andy Porter, Martin Spence and Roy Thompson (Pluto, 1986, £5.95) examines the political and environmental implications of current British energy policies, while the dangers of nuclear energy (with some horrific case studies) are outlined in *Britain's Nuclear Nightmare* by James Cutler and Rob Edwards (Sphere, 1988, £3.99). Again, the positive alternatives are looked at in the next chapter.

The irrepressible Duncan Campbell is the author to read on the military presence in Britain, especially his *War Plan UK* (Paladin, 1982, £2.95) and *The Unsinkable Aircraft Carrier: American Military Power in Britain* (Paladin, 1986, £3.95).

Derrick Mercer and David Puttnam's *Rural England: Our Countryside at the Crossroads* (Macdonald, 1988, £14.95) puts energy resources, military use of the countryside, and much more into the context of the campaign to save England's unique heritage.

The growth of the Greens

It is only very recently that the word green — in relation to politics or lifestyle — has come to mean so much to so many people. In many traditional cultures there has always been a respect for nature and its cycles, and an often unspoken bond of community solidarity and support. After decades in which 'progress', 'growth' and 'competition' have been the watchwords, many people in the supposedly civilised countries are also realising that nobody and nothing can ultimately benefit from a blind adherence to these principles, and that a radical shift of perspective is needed. If we want a healthy and fulfilling future for the planet and all its inhabitants, we need to see, think and act green.

There are three main strands of green philosophy and practice: respect for all life; using resources lightly and appropriately; and acknowledging that everything that happens in the world is connected. That, of course, is only a start, but a useful start.

Another way of distinguishing between different areas of green concern is by their main area of activity. We can distinguish the environmental conservation movement; the organic and wholefood movement; the peace movement; the women's movement; those working in radical health and education; appropriate technology; new economic initiatives; and community action. Each of these movements was thriving well before the concept of

The growth of the Greens

'being green' arose in the late 1970s, but it is now generally accepted that these movements have a great deal in common, and that working together under the general heading of 'green' has many advantages.

Green growth in England

As you will see in the later sections of this chapter, the roots of the English green movement are to be found spreading back many decades, but the recent upsurge of interest can be dated fairly precisely to the late 1960s, when authors like Rachel Carson and Paul Ehrlich, John Barr and Max Nicholson, started alerting people about an impending environmental crisis. This was also the period during which parallel movements like the peace movement and the women's movement experienced a rapid growth of concern, when many communal groups came together and 'back to the land' became a popular rallying cry.

Blueprint for Survival, an early 'green manifesto' published in 1972, engaged the concern of several hundred people who came together to form a network which eventually, after several changes of name, became the Green Party in 1985. Other environmental organisations like Friends of the Earth and Greenpeace experienced rapid growth during the 1970s; together with many other activist organisations, both experienced something of a tailing off of interest in the early 1980s, though concern and active membership are now at an all-time high.

Many people who were involved in the early stirrings of the green movement now feel that although much remains to be done, the movement is well-established and already has many successes to its credit. Public opinion is now firmly behind many green policies, with recent polls showing majorities in favour of recycling waste, abandoning nuclear power, adopting proportional representation, outlawing whaling and putting tight controls on industrial pollution.

The growth of the Greens

Will is one thing, however, and action another. Many green initiatives require legislation and international agreement, but much can be done by individual people, working on their own and in small groups. Since an understanding of connectedness is central to green thinking, it follows that every action we take has consequences for which we are responsible. Every action we take is either for life or against life — there isn't much that is neutral. It's a big responsibility, and even if we choose not to look at it our actions still have consequences which either enhance or detract from the quality of life for all the planet's inhabitants.

One of the aims of the *Green Guide* is to point you, the discriminating traveller, in the direction of those projects which are working to sustain the variety and quality of life in this small country.

The growth of the green movement is explored in Jonathon Porritt and David Winner's *The Coming of the Greens* (Fontana, 1988, £3.95), while you will find a detailed account of the Green Party in Sara Parkin's *Green Parties* (Heretic, 1988, £6.95). For an encyclopedic and very readable guide and overview of everything green in Britain today, get hold of my *Green Pages: A Directory of Natural Products, Services, Resources and Ideas* (Optima, 1988, £9.99) — it includes everything that wouldn't fit in this *Guide*!

Of the various magazines that cover green issues in England (they are all listed in *Green Pages*), look out for *Green Line*, which includes a listing of forthcoming events, and *Environment Now*, part of the monthly magazine *World*, a more mainstream publication though with a progressive edge.

The Green Party in England, which has local groups throughout the country, can be contacted at 10 Station Parade, Balham High Road, London SW12 9AZ. It publishes an excellent bi-monthly newspaper called *Econews*. Friends of the Earth are at 26-28 Underwood Street, London N1 7JQ, and Greenpeace at 30-31 Islington Green, London N1 8XE; both have extensive publications lists and will answer specific environmental queries.

Environmental conservation

Nearly a million people in England belong to one or another of the country's many nature and conservation groups, and this doesn't include another million or so members of the National Trust. Although organisations like the Royal Society for the Protection of Birds and the Society for the Protection of Ancient Buildings go back many decades, the rapid growth of membership of these organisations has been in the last twenty years. Nobody could say that the English weren't at all concerned about conserving their heritage.

If only the response from government, landowners and industry were so enthusiastic. As we have seen in earlier chapters, for every advance made by conservationists a new and ever more menacing threat looms on the horizon. It would be comforting to believe that those in power are starting to listen to those who know and understand just how near the natural environment is to breaking point; will they take heed in time?

Of the many books covering different aspects of conservation, two that will be of particular use to the green traveller are Angela King and Sue Clifford's *Holding Your Ground: An Action Guide to Local Conservation* (Temple Smith, £5.95) (which includes many practical and visitable local conservation initiatives; good contact lists too), and Michael Barker's *Directory for the Environment* (Routledge and Kegan Paul, £15.95 — consult it in a library), which gives addresses, phone numbers and descriptions of nearly 1,400 groups and organisations concerned with the environment.

Wholefoods and the organic movement

1946 saw the foundation of The Soil Association, established to encourage an ecological approach to agriculture; at last food buyers and shops, even supermarkets, are waking up to the inescapable fact that pesticides, additives and complex processing do not make for healthier food. All they do is impoverish the land, boost the medical industry, and 'add value' which is passed on to the consumer in artificially inflated prices.

Alan Gear's *New Organic Food Guide* (Dent, 1987, £3.95) tells you where you can buy organic produce, while Clive Johnstone's *Real Food Shop and Restaurant Guide* (Ebury, 1985, £6.95) will guide you

The growth of the Greens

to the best wholefood shops; the situation is changing rapidly, however, so local information may be more reliable.

Working Weekends on Organic Farms (19 Bradford Road, Lewes, Sussex BN7 1RB) organises visits to organic projects, and has also produced a very useful *Directory of Organizations and Training in the UK Organic Movement* (£1), full of annotated entries with addresses and phone numbers of groups and projects. The Soil Association (86-88 Colston Street, Bristol BS1 5BB) has details of organic farms and smallholdings throughout the country, and will probably be able to point you in the direction of projects that you can visit.

If you are anywhere near Coventry during your travels, don't miss the National Centre for Organic Gardening at Ryton Gardens (see page 108).

The peace movement

For three hundred years the Quakers have been saying no to institutionalised violence; many others declared their pacifism during the two global wars of the twentieth century. It was the horror of nuclear warfare that most stirred the English to protest in the postwar period, with the Campaign for Nuclear Disarmament leading the way.

The women's peace movement, rallying round the courageous peace camps at the missile site at Greenham Common, blossomed during the early 1980s, a period which also saw the willingness of many people to become involved in public acts of civil disobedience.

The best way to contact the peace movement in England is to look out for the fortnightly newspaper *Peace News*, which contains up-to-date details of groups, actions and events. *Housmans Peace Diary* (£3.95) includes addresses of groups throughout the country, while for a more comprehensive listing there is *The International Peace Directory* (Northcote House, 1987, £8.95).

The National Peace Council (29 Great James Street, London WC1N 3ES) acts as the liaison and coordination centre of the British peace movement, and provides a very useful information service. Housman's Bookshop at 5 Caledonian Road, London N1 (very near Kings Cross station) has a comprehensive selection of books about peace and related issues.

The women's movement

The modern women's movement is generally considered to have been born in North America in the mid-1960s; by

1968 the first English women's groups had been formed in London, and the first national Women's Liberation Conference was held in Oxford in 1970.

The women's movement has achieved a great deal in twenty years, including both specific improvements in the standing of women and in attitudes towards questions of practical sexual politics. Yet in many ways little has changed, and at a time of economic and social pressure women are often in danger of losing what gains have been made.

The women's movement has always been decentralised, its groups and contacts short-lived and transient. The best way to make contact with it is probably through the *Spare Rib Diary* (£4.95), which contains detailed resource lists of every aspect of the movement; you can keep up to date with a recent issue of *Spare Rib* or *Everywoman* magazine, both of which have information about upcoming events. A *Women's Peace Directory* (£3.75) is available from Solid Women, Pump Close, Shilton, Oxfordshire OX8 4AB, while *Everywoman* (34a Islington Green, London N1) produces a useful *Directory of Women's Co-operatives and Other Enterprises*.

The two women's bookshops in London are Sisterwrite at 190 Upper Street, Islington, and Silver Moon at 68 Charing Cross Road. A Woman's Place at Hungerford House, Victoria Embankment (Tel: 01-836 6081) provides a useful information service and houses the Feminist Library, which includes a comprehensive resource section.

Paralleling the women's movement, though on a much smaller scale, England also has an active men's movement.

Of several publications, *Men for Change* (106 Welstead Avenue, Aspley, Nottingham NG8 5NS) is a bimonthly newsletter giving details of news, groups and events.

Radical health and education

Many strands have made up this section of the green movement, from holistic health practitioners and radical therapy groups to deschoolers and freeschoolers. Many forms of alternative healing and education are in fact revivals of traditional skills and relationships, having in common the belief that the carer or teacher is in an equal relationship with the client, and that the process should essentially be 'client-centred', rather than the emphasis being on what the professional thinks the client most needs.

Both 'health' and 'education' cover such a broad spectrum that a short description can do them little justice. Suffice to say that they are both fields within which much useful work has been done in experimenting with new and more fulfilling ways of working, and that the mainstream professions have adopted more than they often care to acknowledge from these experiments.

In health, the two national organisations networking in holistic healing are the British Holistic Medical Association (179 Gloucester Place, London NW1 6DX) and the Institute for Complementary Medicine (21 Portland Place, London W1N 3AF). Both are very approachable.

If your interest is in radical psychotherapy, the best source of information is the Association for Humanistic Psychology (12 Southcote Road, London N19 5BJ), which provides an information service, and will suggest a suitable therapist if you need one (the telephone number for referrals is 01-928 7102).

In education it is more difficult to suggest one source for useful information, though a current issue of *Libertarian Education* (The Cottage, The Green, Leire, Leicestershire LE17 5HL) or *Green Teacher* (Llys Awel, 22 Heol Pentrerhedyn, Machynlleth, Powys SY20 8DN, Wales) will contain useful and up-to-date information about projects and forthcoming events. Richard North's *Schools of Tomorrow: Education as if People Mattered* (Green Books, £6.50) includes an account of the well-known Small School at Hartland in Devon, as well as other recent educational experiments.

Appropriate technology

Tools and techniques which are entirely appropriate to the task in hand have been used by traditional societies throughout the ages. It is only because the complex technologies now widespread in the Western world are in many cases so inappropriate that it needed Fritz Schumacher to remind us in the early 1970s that 'small is beautiful'. Since then the concept of appropriate technol-

The growth of the Greens

ogy has been refined and put to work in many different settings, from bicycles to light rail, preventive medicine to wind power.

Schumacher was English (an ex-Coal Board adviser), and so were many of the early initiatives in AT, though you will need to cross the border to Wales to see the highpoint of British AT in action at the renowned Centre for Alternative Technology at Machynlleth.

A good place for AT enthusiasts to start their exploration of England is the Intermediate Technology Bookshop at 103-105 Southampton Row, London WC1 (who also do a very useful catalogue), and the best and most up-to-date AT information (mostly on energy issues though others are touched on) comes in the bi-monthly newsletter of the Network for Alternative Technology and Technology Assessment (NATTA, c/o Energy and Environment Research Unit, Faculty of Technology, The Open University, Walton Hall, Milton Keynes MK7 6AA).

New economics

New economics is the youngest sibling of the green family, having been born in 1983 as a Green Party initiative called The Other Economic Summit, which ran meetings alongside the world summit conferences of 1984 and 1985 and has evolved green-tinted policy on a wide range of economic issues.

Although 'new economics' is a recent arrival, experimental ways of organising work and income have a long history in England. The co-operative movement was founded in Lancashire in 1844, and new co-operatives are now being established at the rate of twenty a month. Businesses owned and run by local communities are also thriving, while many types of economic partnership between local authorities, workers, trade unions and voluntary organisations are being tried.

There are several good periodicals and books which will lead you into green economic initiatives. *New Economics* is produced by the New Economics Foundation (27 Thames House, South Bank Business Centre, 140 Battersea Park Road, London SW11 4NB); Business in the Community (227a City Road, London EC1V 1LX) produce a free magazine and newsletter; and The Centre for

Employment Initiatives (140a Gloucester Mansions, Cambridge Circus, London WC2H 8PA) has an excellent bi-monthly magazine called *Initiatives*.

John Osmond's very readable *Work in the Future* (Thorsons, 1986, £5.99) contains many visitable examples of experimental projects, and a complete directory of co-operatives and community businesses (*The National Directory of New Co-operatives and Community Businesses*, 1986, £5.50) is obtainable from the Co-operative Development Agency (CDA, Broadmead House, 21 Panton Street, London SW1Y 4DR). Guy Dauncey's *After the Crash: The Emergence of the Rainbow Economy* (Green Print, 1988, £6.99) gives a good overview of the field.

Community action

Until very recently it has not been the habit of central and local government in England to ask the inhabitants of a particular area what they really need in the way of housing and services. One Liverpool housing association summed up their city council's approach as 'When we want your opinion, we'll give it to you.'

Things are changing very rapidly, however, as people and communities recognise that they do have the power and can learn the necessary skills to participate in the creation of their own environment. Once one task has been completed successfully, moreover, it shows how much else is possible. Assisted by professional and technical advisers, community-led schemes not only provide people with what they really want; they usually provide employment, save money, and lead to a real sense of co-operation and fulfilment.

The best place to find out about community initiatives in England is the bi-monthly *Community Network*, the joint newsletter of the Association of Community Technical Aid Centres, the Town and Country Planning Association and the Royal Institute of British Architects Community Architecture Group (what a mouthful: write for details to ACTAC, Royal Institution, Colquitt Street, Liverpool L1 4DE). Nick Wates and Charles Knevitt's *Community Architecture* (Penguin, 1987, £4.95) includes details of many schemes and has an impressive resource section, while the Community Technical Aid Centre (11 Bloom Street, Manchester M1 3HS) has produced a useful series of information sheets about community projects throughout the country.

Practical advice

Where to stay

As you travel around England you have several options where accommodation is concerned. Having friends to stay with is almost invariably the pleasantest and cheapest choice, and unlike countries such as the USA and Australia, a full half of all holidays taken by the English are spent staying at the homes of friends or relatives.

An excellent way of meeting friends and finding interesting places to stay is through an organisation called Servas (77 Elm Park Mansions, Park Walk, London SW10 0AP). Members of Servas offer free accommodation to each other in exchange for joining in with whatever activities (usually household or community work) the host is involved with. The time limit for a visit is usually two days, and the scheme is only available to registered Servas members.

The next cheapest form of accommodation, though cost must often be balanced against comfort, is camping. The trend is towards large frame tents put up at organised campsites in the company of large numbers of other holiday-makers, though in most parts of rural England it is not difficult to find a secluded campsite for a night's stopover with a small tent. It is a good idea to ask if you plan to camp anywhere near human habitation, and many farmers (if asked in a friendly way) will suggest an appropriate campsite on their land. Stop in each place only for a short time, take sensible precautions about

Practical advice

looking after your belongings, leave no traces behind you, respect the permanent inhabitants of your chosen site, and you will have few problems camping in England.

You can buy several campsite guides to the country, though there is really no need since any tourist information office will provide campsite details if you need them. For an idea of what the country has to offer to backpackers and lovers of the open-air life, look out for the latest issue of *The Great Outdoors* magazine.

The youth hostel tradition was born in England, and today there is a network of more than 200 hostels in England, particularly thick on the ground in the best walking areas. This is usually the cheapest accommodation that you will find, though it is important to book well ahead if you plan to visit during July and August.

The England and Wales Youth Hostels Association (YHA) *Handbook* can be bought from the YHA, Trevelyan House, 8 St Stephen's Hill, St Albans AL1 2DY. You must be a member of the Association to use the hostels, but you can join at the first hostel you stay at; members of affiliated associations in other countries are welcome to use YHA hostels without further membership payment.

England has a fine tradition of bed and breakfast accommodation, and even at the height of summer you should be able to find a B&B which is pleasant and not too expensive. Prices vary quite a lot; a night in London can easily cost £15, while you should need to pay no more than £9 in many rural areas — unlike many countries, you pay per person rather than per room. For this you will usually get a comfortable bed and as much breakfast as you can eat; if requested, many will provide an evening meal or a packed lunch. All tourist information offices maintain an accommodation register and will find you a suitable B&B, often without charging for the booking service. Larger information offices are linked into the 'book a bed ahead' (BABA) system, whereby they can find

Practical advice

you suitable accommodation almost anywhere in the country; this may involve a small fee.

Hotels in England also offer bed and breakfast, though the extra comfort and service you get rarely compensates for the price you pay, and I imagine few 'green travellers' requiring a well-stocked drinks cabinet or a private golf course. Many hotels now offer cheaper 'mini-breaks' where, especially out of season, two or three day stays cost little more than a single night — regional tourist boards can provide details. There was an attempt in the 1970s to introduce American-style motels to England, but most natives are much too attached to their B&Bs to want the impersonality of such establishments.

There are many guides to hotels and B&B accommodation in England, most of which offer little indication of any special facilities they may offer. A direct approach to a tourist information office, making it clear what you want, will usually produce the best results.

Several organisations produce lists of accommodation providing for special needs, such as vegetarian or vegan food, non-smoking rooms or storage for bicycles. These include:

The International Vegetarian Travel Guide published annually by The Vegetarian Society (Parkdale, Dunham Road, Altrincham, Cheshire WA14 4QG); the 1989-90 edition costs £3.99. The March issue of *The Vegetarian* magazine carries a holiday guide, while a more detailed *Vegetarian Holiday and Restaurant Guide*, compiled by Pauline Davies, is published by Green Print at £2.99.

The Vegan Holiday and Restaurant Guide is published periodically by The Vegan Society (33-35 George Street, Oxford OX1 2AY); the 1988 edition costs £2.50.

Action on Smoking and Health (5-11 Mortimer Street, London W1N 7RH) have details of non-smoking holiday accommodation in England; they will help if you know where you want to visit, and plan to publish a handbook including this information in the near future.

The Cyclists' Touring Club (69 Meadrow, Godalming, Surrey GU7 3HS) produces a members' *Handbook* every two years, which includes lists of bed and breakfast establishments which particularly welcome cyclists.

The Ramblers' Association (1-5 Wandsworth Road, London SW8 2XX) also has a handbook, *The Ramblers' Yearbook*. This annual

Practical advice

publication, available only to members, lists over 2,300 selected B&Bs, and makes membership of the association well worth while for this alone.

The one accommodation guide I can heartily recommend is *The Healthy Holiday Guide* by Catherine Mooney (Headway Publications, 1988, £4.95) — every one of the nearly 200 B&Bs and hotels has been chosen for its friendly service and attention to healthy detail. Most provide vegetarian fare; all understand about wholefoods.

Self-catering accommodation is on the increase in Britain, and this is a good way of arranging a holiday for a group of people if you want to stay in one place for a week at a time.

As in other countries, activity holidays are also becoming very popular, and this can be a very good way to see a new area or try a new activity in the company of like-minded people and knowledgeable teachers. A few communes-cum-workshop-centres in England offer both workshops and B&B type accommodation; you should always check that you will be welcome at such places before you land on their doorstep.

Of several organisations which act as agencies for self-catering accommodation, one of the friendliest and most helpful is Country Holidays, 97 Spring Mill, Earby, Colne, Lancashire BB8 6RN.

For activity holidays one of the best guides is the English Tourist Board's annual *Activity and Hobby Holidays* (£2.50 for the 1989 edition), while if you are looking more for residential educational courses, the National Institute of Adult Continuing Education (19b De Montfort Street, Leicester LE1 7GE) produces an annual booklet (£1.50) listing more than 3,000 summer courses which are open to anybody. If you are planning activity holiday arrangements for a large group, look out for *The Good Stay Guide* (Broadcast Books, 1986, £6.95), which lists hostels and study centres throughout the country.

Many of the communities offering accommodation are listed in *The Healthy Holiday Guide* (see above); for a full list of communes in England, send £1.00 plus a large sae to Communes Network, Lifespan, Townhead, Dunford Bridge, Sheffield S30 6TG. Two English communities offering full workshop programmes (large sae) are Monkton Wyld Court (Charmouth, Bridport, Dorset DT6 6DQ) and Lower Shaw Farm (Shaw, near Swindon, Wiltshire SN5 9PJ).

Practical advice

Getting around

England is quite a small country, and nowhere is more than a day's travel from anywhere else. This is both good news and bad — good because it makes it possible to visit a variety of places in a relatively short time; not so good because there is a temptation to try and get to more different places than is beneficial for you or for England!

England is also a crowded country, which in general means that as you travel you will find yourself in the company of many other travellers, travelling through a densely settled landscape. If you can possibly avoid travelling by car, then do; in urban England and in the more touristed areas during the summer a car is really more trouble than it is worth, quite apart from doing severe environmental damage.

Public transport in England is better than most natives would have you believe. Between the main centres there are frequent train and coach services, and in urban areas public transport (if you can find out about it) is usually frequent and fairly fast. Punctuality of public transport services, with increased pressure from its consumers, has improved in recent years, though services are also — with rare exceptions — very badly co-ordinated.

Despite being mutilated in the 1960s, the country's rail network provides a fast and usually comfortable service to all the country's cities and main towns. Ticket prices are relatively expensive, and since right-wing politicians insist that the British rail network should be the only one in the world not to be government subsidised (while subsidising roads to the hilt), rail fares have been rising far faster than the cost of living.

Free train timetables are available for most routes, and the complete British Rail timetable (a bulky tome) is good value at £3.50. There are number of discount schemes available, including a family railcard and a student railcard — both must be bought in England when you arrive (for details write to British Rail, PO Box

Practical advice

28, York YO1 1FB). Saver tickets are the cheapest return fares, with an additional discount if you can avoid travelling on Fridays and other peak days. If you are visiting England from abroad and know exactly where you want to go, it is always cheaper to buy your rail tickets at the same time as you book your travel to England; there are also special schemes like the BritRail Pass which offer unlimited rail travel within a prearranged period of time — these too must be bought before you leave home.

Nationwide coach services link nearly 2,000 towns and cities — fares are usually around half that of trains, journey times 1½-2 times as long (the fact that it takes nearly twice as much energy to carry a coach passenger as a train passenger proves how much hidden support is given to the country's road system).

Local bus services range from the excellent, through the nondescript, to the nonexistent. Most cities have a good bus service, especially since minibus services were widely introduced in the mid 1980s; several cities have even made moves towards an integrated public transport system involving buses and trains, though this is very much the exception rather than the rule. The availability of clear timetables is improving rapidly, though many operators still make the assumption that you know an area better than most visitors are likely to.

Bus stops in most parts of England (*if* you can find one, and *if* they display any information at all) do not display useful information about the routes they serve; the English could learn a great deal from their Dutch or German counterparts. Where public transport in England is concerned, it is always worth checking and checking again that the bus or train that you are about to board is really going where you want to be.

For information about national bus and coach services in England, write to National Express, 13 Regent Street, London SW1Y 4LR; National Express are by no means the only coach operators, but do run by far the most comprehensive network. For local services you can either ask at tourist information centres or at bus stations; county council public transport departments (passenger transport executives in the conurbations of the North and Midlands) are also good sources of information, especially about arrangements for people with special needs. The entries for individual places later in this guide include information about public transport.

If you are particularly interested in public transport issues, the bi-monthly magazine *On The Move* (from newsagents or from Transit Publications, South Bank Business Centre, 13 Park House, 140 Battersea Park Road, London SW11 4NB) provides up-to-date information, together with a comprehensive resource pullout and a very useful 'fare-check' section. If used wisely, a current copy of *On The Move* could save you a good deal of cash and frustration.

Cycling in England is a pleasant way of seeing the countryside, especially in the summer. Towns and cities, too, are waking up to the bicycle — some, like Oxford, Cambridge and York have invested in a system of cycleways and bike-parking spaces.

The Cyclists' Touring Club (69 Meadrow, Godalming, Surrey GU7 3HS), over a hundred years old, is the country's foremost campaigning group for cyclists. If you plan a cycling holiday it is well worth joining the CTC if only to obtain their excellent *Handbook* and to use their cheap insurance scheme.

Britain's canal system, developed in the late eighteenth and early nineteenth centuries, still provides a transport network for pleasure and commercial use alike. Canals offer a relatively pollution-free way of transporting bulk cargoes around the country, and very pleasant walking along their towpaths.

The British Waterways Board (Melbury House, Melbury Terrace, London NW1 6JX) is the first port of call for anyone interested in England's canals. They produce a wide range of literature, including details of canalboat holidays throughout the country.

Whatever other forms of travel they use during their stay in England, all green travellers should remember that walking is still the most efficient and pollution-free method of travelling short distances, and more and more people are enjoying the challenge and rewards of long-distance walking, too. England is now criss-crossed by a network of trails, with even more planned for the near future.

Practical advice

The Ramblers Association (1-5 Wandsworth Road, London SW8 2XX) can provide a range of services to walkers, including their invaluable *Ramblers' Yearbook* and access to their comprehensive map library. The British Tourist Authority has produced a very useful leaflet called *Walking in Britain* which has details of 52 long-distance routes and addresses of centres which organise walking holidays, while the Countryside Commission (see under 'countryside'), has a leaflet called *Recreational Paths* which lists 72 routes other than the longer trails.

Finally, a word about hitch-hiking in England. Hitching in England is generally both safe and easy, especially away from the cities. Most advice to do with thumbing lifts is common sense: look after yourself, refuse any lift that you don't like the look of, stand in a safe place where vehicles can stop easily, and — most important — look as though you want to go somewhere and you'll be good company.

There are books about hitch-hiking in England, like Ken Lussey's *Hitch-Hikers Guide to Great Britain*, but if you know anything at all about thumbing lifts you won't need a book; just hope that everyone else has read the book so you can stand in a *different* place.

What and where to eat

The English traditionally eat a large breakfast, and unless you make it clear to your hosts that you want something different you will almost certainly be offered a cooked and very non-vegetarian meal as you wander bleary-eyed into the B&B dining room.

One o'clock usually marks the start of lunchtime in England, and throughout the north of the country the midday meal, usually called dinner, was traditionally the main meal of the day, followed by a farinaceous tea at around five o'clock in the afternoon. More and more people now follow the southern non-working-class style, eating a light meal at lunchtime and having their main meal in the early evening, usually between six and eight o'clock. Thus while 'tea' in the north tends to mean a full

Practical advice

meal, in the south it suggests a cup of tea and a plate of cucumber sandwiches.

Many restaurants, especially of the fast food variety, now open throughout the day. If you want to be certain of a proper meal, however, it is best to find somewhere to eat between 12 noon and 2pm (for lunch) or 6pm and 9pm (for an evening meal). If you know in advance where you would like to eat, it is well worth reserving a table, especially on Friday and Saturday evenings and at the height of summer.

Until the early 1960s, eating out in England usually meant either an elegant restaurant, out of the financial reach of most people, or a commercial dining room which reflected the domestic eating patterns of the bulk of the population. American-style fast food chains introduced the hamburger and the hotdog, but these have never ousted the traditional — and infinitely healthier — fish bars. Chinese and Indian restaurants, reflecting the postwar immigration boom, are still much more widespread than Big Macs and their lookalikes, and the quality and variety of the food they offer has improved enormously since their early days.

Today it is hard to tell whether things are improving or not. You can certainly find wholefood meals more easily, and there are usually vegetarian alternatives, but most pubs and cafés are still producing pre-cooked meals out of packets and tins, cooked under the microwave. Restaurants which use only fresh ingredients are worth remembering.

Good beers, ales and ciders are the traditional drinks to accompany your lunchtime bread and cheese or to hold while you while away an evening at the local hostelry. 'Real ale' is now a Big Thing in England, and once you've tasted it you are unlikely to be satisfied with watery fizzy beer out of a can (heaven forbid that you should even consider buying anything in a can!). Real ale is not hard to find these days, though do try to drink the local ales — you'll be pleasantly surprised at the flavour and the variety as well as being amused by names like Christmas Noggin and Witches Brew.

There are two outstanding guides to eating out cheaply and heathily in England. *The Real Food Shop and Restaurant Guide* (Ebury, 1985, £6.95) has the additional attraction of including good wholefood shops, and the descriptions are full and accurate, if a little dated in some cases. *Cheap Eats* (Hodder and Stoughton, annual, £5.95) is not so wholefood oriented and its entries are less reliable, but it is more comprehensive and up-to-date than *The Real Food Guide*.

For vegetarians *the* handbook is *The International Vegetarian Travel Guide* (£4.99 from The Vegetarian Society, Parkdale, Dunham Road, Altrincham, Cheshire WA14 4QG), while Sarah Brown's *Vegetarian London* (Thorsons, 1988, £3.50) gives all the information you could possibly need as a vegetarian in the capital city. Similar information for vegans is contained in *The Vegan Holiday and Restaurant Guide* (£2.50 from The Vegan Society, 33-35 George Street, Oxford OX1 2AY).

The Real Ale movement in England is spearheaded by the Campaign for Real Ale (CAMRA, 34 Alma Road, St Albans AL1 3BW), who publish the annual *Good Beer Guide* (the 1989 edition costs £5.95) and *Good Cider Guide* (£4.95). Each contains detailed information about breweries and where you can buy their brews.

What to take with you

'As little as possible' should be your motto: the theory is simple, the practice less so.

Around your person, preferably in a zipped pocket, keep money, passport, tickets, your travel plans and timetables for the day. In an easily accessible place have the map, your current book for reading during unplanned delays, and your address book and diary. This is enough equipment for a day's outing, provided you dress appropriately before you set out.

If you take lightweight cotton clothes, a couple of sweaters and several pairs of warm socks, and wear your heaviest coat or anorak when travelling so it doesn't take up luggage space, your clothing shouldn't take up too much space, especially if you are travelling in summer. A

Practical advice

good pair of trainers and a pair of sandals should be sufficient footwear unless you plan some rough mountain walking; rubber wellies can usually be provided by your country friends who invite you to wade through the mud with them.

You can often leave at least part of your luggage with friends while you travel, and you can always post some of it home if you know you won't need it again on this trip.

There are a growing number of places where you can hire camping equipment, so unless you have very lightweight equipment or are planning to spend most of your time under canvas, check carefully whether you need to take your own stuff. Modern camping equipment is very compact and light, as are today's rucksacks; on the other hand, a rucksack can sometimes be much more of a nuisance than a soft bag unless you actually plan to carry it on your back most of the time. There is quite a temptation to fill a large rucksack 'just because it's there'.

When planning what to carry with you, it is always useful to have the ultimate green question at the back of your mind: 'Do I *really* need it?'

The best maps of England are produced by the Ordnance Survey (Information and Enquiries, Ordnance Survey, Southampton SO9 4DH), who will gladly send you a copy of their complete catalogue. The Routemaster maps cover England in 6 sheets at 1:250,000, and are excellent for travelling by public transport or bicycle. If you are walking in a particular area, you will want the relevant Landranger maps; these cover England in 122 sheets at 1:50,000. Even more detailed are the Pathfinder 1:25,000 maps: it takes more than 800 of these to cover the country. OS maps are not cheap, but they are detailed, accurate and a delight to look at.

Many regions and towns produce very good basic guides to their areas, and you can nearly always get a simple local map free from any tourist information office.

Clothing, camping equipment and many of the other things you may need on your travels are relatively cheap in England compared with most European countries, and similar to those in the USA, another reason for not carrying around more than you really need.

Practical advice

Health

Travelling can be exhilarating and stimulating, but it can also be tiring and stressful. It is important to look after yourself on your travels, and to make sure that the healthy stimulation isn't negated by too much physical and emotional angst. Give yourself time to relax and calm down from time to time, treat your body to a healthy diet and some exercise in the fresh air, and you should have few if any health problems.

If, despite looking after yourself, you are feeling under the weather, there are a number of things you can do. Most chemists' shops in England will have a qualified pharmacist on hand to suggest an appropriate remedy, and many will carry a range of homeopathic (and perhaps even some herbal) remedies.

There are an ever-increasing number of practitioners of complementary medical techniques of one kind or another, and it is getting easier to find them too, since several national umbrella organisations have referral services. Most wholefood and alternative book shops have a noticeboard which will almost certainly point you in the direction of local practitioners.

The British National Health Service, set up in 1946, provides a comprehensive medical service to everyone normally resident in the country; there are also reciprocal arrangements with health services in other countries. If you have an accident or are suddenly taken ill, there will usually be no hesitation in providing you with the facilities you need; the emergency services are on the whole excellent. On the other hand, the NHS is very drugs-and-surgery oriented, and has been dubbed the National Illness Service by some observers, since along with the medical establishment throughout the Western world it still seems to be more interested in symptoms and cures than in health and preventatives.

It is hard to know what to advise where health insurance is concerned; the whole idea of putting cash values

Practical advice

to lost lives and limbs is anathema to most green-thinkers, yet if a drunken driver should take aim at you it will be at least a little comfort that the insurance company will get you home without your having to fork out. Think carefully about your priorities and responsibilities before you buy travel insurance, then get some good professional advice.

The Institute for Complementary Medicine (21 Portland Place, London W1N 3AF) runs a telephone referral service on 01-636 9543, and has plans for a comprehensive guide to holistic practitioners in Britain. The ICM also operates a regional 'public information point' service; regional telephone numbers within this service are given later in the guide under particular regions. If you suddenly find yourself in need of a good therapist or counsellor, the Association for Humanistic Psychology operates a similar referral service, with more than 300 practitioners on their register; the number is 01-928 7102.

If you are not British and need the services of the NHS, the bureaucratic details will usually be dealt with automatically; if you are interested in knowing in advance what reciprocal medical arrangements exist between your country and Britain, you can write for a leaflet to DHSS (Leaflets), PO Box 21, Stanmore, Middlesex HA7 1AY.

In an emergency, simply dial 999 from the nearest telephone — the call is free — and ask for an ambulance. Speed is often vital, especially if someone has lost consciousness.

Language and dialect

The English are notoriously bad at learning other people's languages, but since so many English people now go to Europe for their holidays, perhaps they are getting better at listening carefully and trying to understand what is needed; younger people especially will even sometimes try to use their French or German.

Nearly two million people living in England speak a second 'mother tongue', and any visitor to England who speaks a language shared by many immigrants to the country such as Hindi, Gujarati or Cantonese will find these languages in everyday use in areas with a sizeable ethnic population.

Practical advice

Many parts of England have retained at least something of their regional dialects, and a traveller cannot fail to notice the range of accents from the round 'oi's of the south-west to the near-Scots of Northumberland. If English is not your first language you may sometimes find it hard to understand what is being said to you. Many English people are quite patient, however: another English trait is perseverance; once they know you have something to say, they won't give up without a struggle!

Money

Most English people, especially outside the big cities, are still very trusting about money. You will not have to pay for a meal or a night's accommodation until you leave, and the chances are that if you should drop your wallet someone will notice and hand it back to you.

The sort of person reading this guide will probably never need to carry large amounts of cash; travellers' cheques and/or a credit card will be accepted in a wide range of places, including railway stations. Do remember that many British banks have a strange habit of closing at 3.30pm, and that post offices close on Saturday afternoons.

If you are a resident of the EEC, you can earn money in England quite legitimately, and some long-term travellers finance their travels by taking seasonal work. Residents of other countries should technically have a work permit to work in England, though you can always barter your work in exchange for accommodation or travel. You can also negotiate skills exchanges — I'll help you to harvest your vegetables if you'll give me a massage. None of this is illegal; there are many ways of conducting exchanges which involve no cash.

Approaching people and organisations

In general you will find that people are delighted if you show an interest in their pet project; even more delighted

Practical advice

if you offer to help. There are a few commonsense considerations, however, which will help you to make the most of the contacts you make during your travels:

— Be discriminating about the contacts you make, and be as clear as possible about what you want. If you are interested in visiting organic herb gardens, for example, it will almost certainly be more productive to write individual letters to three or four, explaining your interest and experience, than to send a standard photocopied letter to every herb-growing member of the Soil Association.

— Always (unless the organisation you are writing to is a public body or a large commercial business) enclose either a stamped self-addressed envelope or envelope re-use label, or an international reply coupon. Most green-tinted organisations do not have the resources to support large postage bills.

— If you plan to visit (unless your planned port of call is recognised tourist attraction), always give advance notice. Writing well ahead is best, though since people are not always very good at replying, it is a good idea to check the arrangement by phone a day or two ahead of your visit.

— Try to be sensitive to the needs of the people and project you are visiting. Many people involved in greenish activities are good and fascinating talkers, especially when they encounter people as enthusiastic as they are about their pet project, but they do tend to lead busy and unpredictable lives — and they can occasionally become 'green bores', whose only interest seems to be wood-burning stoves or the sex life of bees. You will need to use your judgement!

— If you stay for meals or are driven round a project — anything that involves expense on your host's part — do at least check whether payment is in order. Small and appropriate gifts will almost always be appreciated, especially a little cash help with the project.

If you go about things in the right way you will almost always be welcome to visit green initiatives. But you can't

Practical advice

expect to be cossetted in the way that organised coach parties are. It must be said that greenish people are often not very efficient at responding to enquiries, and the hard work and frequent frustration of getting alternative projects off the ground often impinges on the friendly helpfulness.

Travelling with children

Travelling with children can be tiring and limiting, but it needn't be. You will almost certainly need to plan more in advance, making bookings on public transport and ensuring in good time that you have somewhere to stay — the book a bed ahead scheme (see page 48) is very useful in this respect. In some ways having children with you makes things easier: you can travel by train on a family railcard, for example, and you will probably find it easier to make contact with local people through your shared interest in children. Children will almost inevitably alter the pace of your travelling, slowing you down in some places, speeding you up in others. Given planning, flexibility, and a light touch, however, you can help to make your travels a worthwhile experience for everybody.

A very useful book to have with you if you are travelling with children is Betty Jerman's *Kids' Britain* (Pan, 1986, £2.95), full of places and ideas   things to see and do. Like the *Green Guide*, it divides the country into tourist board areas. There is also a companion volume called *Kids' London* by Elizabeth Holt and Molly Perham (Pan, 1985, £2.95). The Royal Society for Nature Conservation (see page 28) has a junior wing called Watch, which organises events for children all over the country; the local conservation trust (addresses given in the 'wildlife' sections for each region) will be able to supply details. Tourist information offices will often be able to tell you about local events arranged for children.

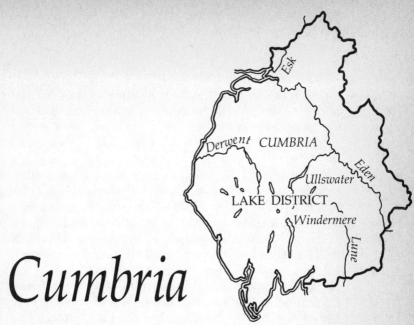

Cumbria

For most travellers, Cumbria begins at Kendal (if approached from the south) or Carlisle (from the north). There is a great deal to be said, however, for coming to the region along the threatened rail route from Settle to Carlisle, when your first glimpse of Cumbria will be the wild unspoilt valley of Mallerstang, or over Melmerby Fell from Alston, from where on a clear day the panorama of the Lakeland peaks is breathtaking.

The Lake District, a compact cartwheel of lakes and mountains no more than thirty miles across, is the heart of

Cumbria

the region, though Cumbria also incorporates a sizeable chunk of the Yorkshire Dales National Park and no less than three areas of outstanding natural beauty — the Solway coast, the north Pennines in the east, and the intimate wooded coastline of Arnside overlooking Morecambe Bay. Though Windermere and Keswick can be crowded torture on a fine summer weekend, the fells are always nearby. The main walking routes have often been trodden to yard-wide scars, but if you avoid the most popular paths you will easily find moors and valleys uncluttered with other people, even at the height of the season. Go a little further afield, to the massive Howgill Fells in the east or the country north of the Roman Wall, and you can walk all day without seeing a soul.

Tourism and traditional hill farming are rural Cumbria's economic mainstays, but the region also has a very long industrial history, from the neolithic stone axe 'factories' of Langdale to the immense and sinister bulk of the Sellafield nuclear site. The Lake District contains more actively protected landscape than any other part of England (the National Trust owns more than a quarter of the park's area), yet environmental threats are ever present, from the pressure of tourism to unsightly mineral extraction, inappropriate afforestation to rural dereliction.

The best time to visit Cumbria is between October and May, when you will find the hills and valleys full of colour and relatively empty of people. You may even see something of how these friendly northern communities operate when they're not working flat out to service the incessant flow of summer tourists.

Regional Tourist Office: Cumbria Tourist Board, Ashleigh, Holly Road, Windermere, Cumbria LA23 2AS (Tel: 096 62 4444).

Ancient Sites: One of the country's finest and largest stone circles, Long Meg and Her Daughters, stands above the River Eden near Salkeld. Long Meg herself stands twelve feet high, and 'tis said that if you break a piece off her she will bleed — don't try. The stone circle at Castlerigg near Keswick is in a superb setting. The fine fifteenth century stone bridge at Kirkby Lonsdale is said to have

Cumbria

been built by the devil when he lost a bet with a local woman — if you look carefully you can see his fingermarks on the coping stone of the second recess on the right as you look towards Casterton.

Trees and Woodland: Until public outcry halted their progress, vast conifer tracts threatened many Cumbrian valleys. As it is, only Ennerdale in the Lakes and the far north-east of the region have been swathed in dense plantations of sitka spruce, which destroys the ground flora and is home to a very limited range of bird and insect life. The extensive deciduous woodlands of southern Lakeland, on the other hand, support a rich and varied wildlife, best seen at Arnside Knot (nature trail, leaflet available), Bardsea Country Park near Dalton-in-Furness, and Roundsea Wood near Grange-over-Sands (leaflet available). The woods in Borrowdale, besides adding a unique beauty to an exquisite corner of Cumbria, are considered to be of international importance for their flora and birdlife.

Wildlife: Because the region encompasses a wide variety of habitats, its plant and animal life is extremely rich. Large colonies of breeding seabirds frequent the Solway and Morecambe Bay mudflats; lakes and streams sometimes contain rare glacial relict species like the char and whitefish. The mountain slopes provide a refuge for ravens and falcons, while a few wild red deer and pine marten still survive in the wilder areas. The Cumbria Trust for Nature Conservation (Church Street, Ambleside LA22 0BU) can provide further information.

Protected Areas: The Lake District is England's only mountainous national park, and one of the first to be designated in 1951; it has also been proposed as a World Heritage Site. Nearly 15% of the park, a uniquely high proportion, has been designated as being of special scientific importance. The National Park Visitor Centre at Brockhole near Windermere, set in beautiful landscaped gardens, houses an impressive exhibition about the history and landscape of the park; the centre also hosts a wide range of other activities, while the Terrace Cafeteria is well-known for its local specialities.

The Yorkshire Dales National Park, designated in 1954, straddles the Pennine Hills; some of its wildest and most rugged landscape is found in the region's south-east corner. The mudflats of the Solway Coast were the first part of the region to be designated an Area of Outstanding Natural Beauty, followed by Arnside and Silverdale and, most recently, the area of the Pennines adjoining the Yorkshire Dales National Park.

Access to the Countryside: The Lake District is the most accessible area of England for the walker, more than 40% being in public ownership; elsewhere in the region access to open ground is generally not difficult. There is a wide choice of walker's guides to the most-frequented areas, from the leaflets produced by the Lake District National Park Service to the seven volumes of the detailed and lovingly-illustrated *Pictorial Guide to the Lakeland Fells* by the irrepressible Alfred Wainwright. Shops throughout the region will provide you with more than enough choice.

Organic Initiatives: One of the highlights of small-scale wholefooding in England is the Watermill at Little Salkeld near Penrith. Open every weekday, the shop sells a wide range of organic produce, and Salkeld-milled wholewheat flour is distributed throughout Northern England and the south of Scotland. Well worth a visit.

Local Building Traditions: Geologically speaking, The Lake District is a dome of volcanic and sedimentary rocks surrounded by a limestone rim; the limestone extends eastwards into Northumbria and Yorkshire. The underlying rocks are mirrored in the stone used for houses and field walls alike: hard volcanic rocks and slates in Lakeland; pale limestone and the widespread use of stone roofs elsewhere. Cobble, clay and thatch find their way into the north of the region, while brick is common in the Victorian city of Carlisle. The lively Museum of Lakeland Life and Industry at Kendal shows traditional techniques of building and interior decoration.

Museums: As well as the Lakeland Museum in Kendal (see under 'local building traditions'), two other museums are well worth a visit. Townend, a 'yeoman farmer's' house at Troutbeck, has been preserved by the National Trust to show the past of Lakeland life in a very immediate way. Stott Park Bobbin Mill near Newby Bridge, built in 1835, has been restored by English Heritage to become a working industrial museum.

Craft Workshops: Souvenir shops are thick on the ground in the main centres; only Ambleside has a real 'craft centre' at Zefirelli's Arcade in Compstone Road, where you will find makers of jewellery, pure wool knitwear, pottery and stoneware, as well as an excellent vegetarian pizzeria and the region's best cinema. The tiny village of Dent, high up in the eastern dales, also has a craft centre displaying the work of local craftspeople (excellent teas as well).

At Daffiestown Rigg, Longtown, Hedgerow Baskets make traditional English willow baskets, while at the other end of the region, Candlemakers of Hill Foot, Cark-in-Cartmel, make beautiful hand-sculpted candles. Barnhowe Spinning at Elterwater near Ambleside offers half-day training sessions, an excellent way to learn this traditional craft.

Cumbria

Long-Distance Paths: The Cumbria Way is a valley route through the Lake District from Ulverston to Carlisle, while the Dales Way runs from Ilkley in Yorkshire to Bowness-on-Windermere; there are guidebooks available for both routes. Shorter and easier is the Allerdale Ramble from Seathwaite in Borrowdale to the coast at Maryport, then northwards along the coast to Skinburness (booklet from Allerdale District Council, Cockermouth CA13 0DW).

Energy Initiatives

Nuclear and Anti-Nuclear: At Sellafield nuclear power station and reprocessing plant on the Cumbrian coast, you are invited (according to the brochure) 'to enter an atmospheric journey into the world of nuclear technology' in their multi-million pound visitor centre, but you'll look in vain for information about marine pollution and leukaemia clusters. For this you'll need a copy of James Cutler and Rob Edwards' *Britain's Nuclear Nightmare* which, among other horrors, chronicles Britain's worst nuclear accident, when the Cumbrian reactor caught fire in the heady and secretive days of 1957. The local anti-nuclear campaigning group, Cumbrians Opposed to a Radioactive Environment, can be contacted at 98 Church Street, Barrow-in-Furness.

Alternative Energy: There are few working watermills remaining in Cumbria. Little Salkeld (see 'organic initiatives') is one; another is the picturesque Muncaster Mill, alongside the Ravenglass Railway between Millom and Whitehaven. Both sell wholewheat flour and allow you to see the internal mill workings.

Health: There are few practitioners of complementary medicine in the region, though the Buddhist centre at Conishead Priory, Ulverston (worth a visit in its own right; Tel: 0229 54029) does offer a limited range of healing techniques, including acupuncture and massage. Unless you are really ill, a walk in the hills is likely to be more healing than most conventional treatments.

Transport: Rail services in the region are fairly good, especially if the Carlisle-Settle line remains open. Public road transport is provided by CMS Cumberland (timetables from CMS, Tangier Street, Whitehaven CA28 7XF), and by a number of smaller operators, some of which (like Mountain Goat) run minibus services on the less-used routes.

Worth a visit is the South Tyneland Railway, a narrow-gauge line built on the railbed of the British Rail service to Alston when it was withdrawn; the Ravenglass and Eskdale Railway ('Ratty') in the west combines industrial archaeology with another relatively environmentally-sound visitor attraction.

Cumbria

The many hills make this difficult cycling country, though bikes can be hired from Windermere, Bowness, Keswick and Penrith (ask tourist information offices for details).

Food: Local freshwater fish are one local speciality (don't trust sea fish from the Irish Sea — it's the most radioactive sea in the world); traditional cakes another: try the 'passion cake' if you can find it. If you eat meat, local hill-raised lamb and venison are tasty and relatively ecologically sound.

Bookshops: As far as I know, there are no especially green-tinted bookshops in Cumbria, though it is well worth knowing about Michael Moon's excellent secondhand and antiquarian bookshop at 41-43 Roper Street, Whitehaven. Bookish travellers travel many miles to spend hours browsing more than a mile of shelves; a good balance to the hours spent on the hills, and an excellent way to use a rainy day.

Northumbria

Even two hundred years ago, much of the northern part of this region was still an unsettled semi-wilderness, a debateable land claimed by rival families and subject to cross-border raids. It is still the most sparsely-populated part of England, as walkers of the northern part of the Pennine Way will find. Apart from low-flying jets and cannon fire from the Otterburn ranges, seekers of real peace and quietness will usually find their prayers answered in the rolling Cheviots and along the quiet beaches of Northumberland.

Further south, open landscapes give way to a more enclosed and domestic scene. The ancient county of

Durham, presided over by the dramatic pile of its Gothic cathedral, was a beacon of relative peace and great learning for many centuries, and Durham City is still an important centre of original thinking — the idiosyncratic ecologist David Bellamy and the outspoken Bishop of Durham both hail from the region.

The whole of the south-east corner of the region changed drastically in the century following the industrial revolution. By the 1914-18 war, hardly a valley in Durham was without its branch railway and rows of brick or stone terraces. The 1920s slump hit the region hard, and Jarrow on Tyneside is remembered as much for its marchers as for Bede's monastery. By the 1950s the rot had set in: 'Sunderland had become nondescript;' writes author Thomas Sharp, 'Darlington ditto; Old Hartlepool a ruin; North Shields almost derelict; Morpeth vulgarised.' Of the seventy coalpits working in Northumberland in 1948, only one now remains.

Much of this corner of Northumbria still bears the scars of dereliction, both of landscape and community. Brave experiments in housing and reclamation often stand alongside post-industrial eyesores, but because the North East has been so downtrodden for so long, community self-help of the best kind has blossomed in many areas. Yuppiedom has come to a few suburbs of Newcastle, but for genuineness and down-to-earthness of both place and people, Northumbria is hard to beat.

NEWCASTLE UPON TYNE

Few travellers stay long in Newcastle, though many pass through on their way to somewhere else. Much of the city centre has been vandalised by concrete block developers and urban motorway builders — the Eldon Square monstrosity is one of the largest covered shopping centres in Europe, rivalled only by the new Metro Centre in Gateshead. Luckily they stopped short of Grey Street and the impressive Central Station, but by then there wasn't much left.

The urban developers also had a good bash at Newcastle's suburbs too, occasionally with a glimmer of imagination, as the famous technicolour 'Byker Wall' scheme testifies. By the late seventies, however, the city's inhabitants had had enough and the coffers were running low, so that in recent years Newcastle and the surrounding towns have become a seedbed of self-help experiments in housing and employment provision. The city is one of the country's leaders in energy efficiency, and the recently completed Metro light rail scheme is a model of imaginative public service provision.

If you are prepared to look quite hard for the real Newcastle, and this does mean getting out of the concrete and neon jungle, you will find both pioneering projects and helpful people to tell you about them.

Tourist Information Offices: Central Library, Princess Square (Tel: 091 261 0691); Blackfriars Centre, Monk Street (Tel: 091 261 5367).

Wholefood Restaurants: The natural choices in the city centre are The Super Natural at 2 Princess Square or, if you like Indian, the Rupali at 6 Bigg Market. For coffee, cakes and salads, the Dance City Coffee Shop in Peel Street is worth a visit.

Wholefood Shops: The most right-on place for wholefoods is Mandala Wholefoods at 43 Manor House Road, in the northern university suburb of Jesmond — an excellent range, especially of breads.

Bookshops: No especially green-tinted bookshops; you'll need to go to Alleycat, 15 miles away in Durham, for a decent range, though David Bell's bookshop on Gosforth High Street is worth a browse.

Museums: Nothing particularly exciting, though on a wet day the Blackfriars Centre in Monk Street (history of the city) and the Hancock at Barras Bridge (natural history) are both worth seeing, as is the Museum of Science and Technology in Blandford Street. If you like your industrial archaeology 'on the ground', Tyne and Wear County Council have produced an excellent three-part guide to The Heritage Way, a seventy-mile walk through the countryside around Newcastle, passing old collieries and waggonways, mills and bridges.

Shops and Crafts: The Third World 'equal-partners' trading organisation, Traidcraft, is based in nearby Gateshead. Traidcraft has a city centre Tradefair shop in Carliol Square, selling a wide range of merchandise. At The Makers at Blackfriars, in Stowell Street, is a co-operatively run shop selling local crafts.

City Wildspaces: The city has always enjoyed access to open space, notably the thousand windswept acres of the Town Moor, site of one of England's largest fairs, held in June. Tawny owls and kestrels have nested on the Moor. The local council has also been a pioneer in urban industrial reclamation projects, restoring nearly two thousand acres in the last fifteen years. At the small scale, see the Benwell Nature Park at Atkinson Road, Benwell, or the Walkergate Wildlife Garden at Walkergate School, Coutts Road (school hours only). On the larger scale, Tyne and Wear County Council have produced an excellent series of leaflets to their country parks and nature trails, including the Tyne Riverside Country Park and the Gibside Estate. There is a well-established city farm at Stepney Bank, Byker.

Transport: The Tyne and Wear Metro is the nearest thing in Britain to an urban tramway system, and passenger figures have far surpassed the wildest expectations as the little yellow railcars have caught the public imagination. Fast, frequent, cheap and relatively pollution-free, the Metro is a model for other English cities.

Cycling is not a traditional North-East activity, though the local Tyne Bikes campaign (14 Victoria Avenue, Forest Hall) is working hard for cycleways in the city, and the local branch of the Cyclists' Touring Club (15 Wallington Court, Killingworth) has produced route sheets for several circular rides in the area. Bikes can be hired from Glenbar Hire, 217 Jesmond Road, who also have six other cycle-hiring branches in Northumberland.

Energy Initiatives: Newcastle is the home of two nationally-successful energy conservation organisations, both of which welcome visitors with advance notice. Neighbourhood Energy Action, at 2-4 Bigg Market, pioneered local energy saving schemes, of which there are now more than 250 in Britain; Energy Inform, at 5 Charlotte Square, provides advice and information about energy saving projects. Byker Reclamation Plant at 304 Walker Road is a pioneering 'warmth from waste' project, converting domestic and trade refuse into recyclable raw materials and fuel pellets; it can be visited with advance notice.

Community Initiatives: Byker, an eastern suburb of Newcastle, was the scene in 1968 of one of the country's first experiments in community architecture; walk round the area behind the 'Byker Wall' and see what you think. There are now several successful community landscaping schemes in operation.

Co-operative working is also a growing area in the city, with more than two dozen companies being established in the last ten years, from wholefood shops to the company operating leisure cruises on the River Tyne. The Ouseburn Warehouse Co-op is a converted whiskey warehouse which now houses workshops, studios, the offices of a theatre group, and rehearsal space; started in 1980, it was a pioneering community economic initiative.

Health: There is no centre for complementary medicine in the city, but the Institute for Complementary Medicine contact number (for information about local practitioners and services) is 091 281 1653.

Local Directories: The North-East Environmental Network has produced an excellent local directory called *Green Leaves* — look out for it in libraries. For information about events in the city, consult the bimonthly *On The Town*.

THE REST OF THE REGION

Regional Tourist Office: Northumbria Tourist Board, Aykley Heads, Durham DH1 5UX (Tel: 091 384 6905).

Ancient Sites: Hadrian's Wall, built nearly two thousand years ago to keep the 'barbarians' away from the Roman Empire, can be traced right across central Northumbria and westwards into Cumbria. The eight miles from Greenhead to Housesteads Fort, most of which runs along craggy hilltops, is particularly spectacular, while the Vindolanda fort at Chesterholm shows what the wall might have looked like when it was newly-built. The northern part of the Northumberland coast is rich in antiquities and folklore, especially the 'holy island' of Lindisfarne (approachable only at low tide), and the restored Bamburgh Castle which overlooks the island from the mainland. In a cave under the castle the Laidley Worm — a young bride spellbound by a jealous rival — is said to dwell; a painting in the castle retells the story.

Trees and Woodland: The north of England's largest forest is at Kielder in north Northumberland, where Northumbrian Water have also built a massive reservoir. Aware of the tourist potential, both forest and water authorities have opened visitor centres, which have information about guided walks, cycle and boat hire, and forest ecology. Much of Kielder consists of single-species stands of spruce and fir, devoid of beauty and of wildlife, though there has recently been some sensitive replanting. Further south, the Plessey Woods Country Park near Bedlington and Castle Eden Dene near the 'new town' of Peterlee both offer nature trails (leaflets available) through wooded valleys, while Hamsterley Forest near Bishop Auckland sensitively incorporates beech and birchwoods within the conifer plantations — you may also see roe deer and red squirrels, maybe even a badger.

Wildlife: From the high windswept Cheviot Hills to the coastal sand-dunes of Northumberland and lush river valleys of the Durham coast, Northumbria displays a remarkable variety of habitats. The region contains several very nationally important nature reserves, which are in turn quite different from each other. Birdwatchers come from all over the world to see the seabirds of the Farne Islands, while the valley woodlands conserve important native tree species — oak, ash, alder and juniper. The moorlands have pockets of wildlife found nowhere else in the country: Upper Teesdale has a unique arctic-alpine ecology, well explained by the displays and leaflets at the Bowlees information centre near the spectacular waterfall at High Force. Washington Waterfowl Park, administered by the new town's corporation, is an important staging post for large numbers of migrating birds. More information can be obtained from the Durham County Conservation Trust at 52 Old Elvet, Durham, and the Northumberland Wildlife Trust, based at the Hancock Museum in Newcastle, which has produced a useful membership pack giving details of all its reserves.

Protected Areas: The Northumberland National Park, designated in 1956, includes the wildest parts of western Northumberland. It has a human population of less than 2,500, being very much the land of the sheep and the golden plover, which breeds here. Although a national park, access to many areas is impossible because of the activities of the Forestry Commission and the army, who between them own nearly half of the land in the park. You can get more information about the park from tourist information offices or from the Park Committee at Eastburn, South Park, Hexham. The Cheviot Hills are more interesting than might appear at first sight, since they harbour many 'hidden valleys' — Wooler is an excellent base for exploring these hills.

Almost the whole of the north Northumberland coast has been designated a Heritage Coast, which provides some protection against harmful development; further information can be obtained from Northumberland County Council Planning Department at County Hall, Morpeth.

Access to the Countryside: Access to the moorland not owned by the Ministry of Defence and the Forestry Commission is usually not difficult, though being a remote area not much visited by walkers, you cannot expect to find well-trodden footpaths away from the main routes. The Pennine Way crosses the west of the

Northumbria

region from north to south, and there are plans for a long-distance path along the line of Hadrian's Wall from coast to coast.

Organic Initiatives: Of a handful of organic growers in the region, the most visitable are Eggleston Hall farm at Eggleston near Barnard Castle, and Down to Earth at Nether Warden, Hexham (by appointment only), both of which produce a wide range of fruit and vegetables in season. While not strictly organic, Southwick Village Farm near Sunderland is an important community initiative, designed to interest a wide cross-section of local people in all things agricultural and horticultural, while Cleveland Farm Link (Bishopsmill School, Mill Lane, Norton, Stockton-on-Tees TS20 1LG) exists to foster links between farmers and local residents.

Local Building Traditions: Until the later nineteenth century, local stone was the almost universal building material of the region: limestone in the west, gritstones and sandstones in the east. Escomb's Anglo-Saxon church near Bishop Auckland and the mighty cathedral at Durham — 'half church of God, half castle 'gainst the Scot' — show the effective use of local stone at both ends of the religious spectrum. Thousands of red brick colliery houses were hastily built during the industrial revolution, and brick is still a very common building material in the urbanised parts of Northumbria. The Open Air Museum at Beamish and Preston Hall Museum at Stockton (see below) both incorporate traditional buildings, and a dozen or so towns and villages have produced 'town trail' leaflets, available from local tourist information offices. The Durham County Council pack (£1.10 from The Planning Department, County Hall, Durham) covers seven towns and villages, including Staindrop, attractively ranged around an extensive green once used for protecting livestock during cattle raids, and the beautiful Pennine town of Middleton-in-Teesdale.

Museums: The region has some excellent museums, of which the Beamish Open Air Museum between Chester-le-Street and Stanley is one of the best in Britain. Here you can see trams, restored buildings, craftspeople plying their trade — a real and lasting impression of a way of life which was far more community-based and economically stable than anything we now seem able to produce. Of the many other museums in the region, Stockton's Preston Hall Museum has a Victorian shopping street; the Hunday Countryside Museum at Stocksfield in Northumberland has an enormous range of traditional farm machinery; and the Darlington Railway Museum houses the Locomotion, England's first steam locomotive. Stanhope in Weardale is the home of The Leadmining Centre, an attractive open air museum giving a

Northumbria

good idea of the industrial history of the area, and the Grace Darling Museum at Bamburgh, whatever you think about Victorian romanticism, is one of the country's few museums to commemorate the life and times of a woman.

Craft Workshops: The region's best display of craft work is to be seen at the Northumbria Craft Centre in Bridge Street, Morpeth, where more than forty workers show products ranging from pottery to jewellery. Earthcare, at 33 Saddler Street in Durham, stocks an impressive range of wooden toys, recycled paper products, window transparencies and Third World crafts.

Community Initiatives: At Allenheads, near Hexham, residents have initiated a project to save their declining village. Supported by a national community projects fund, the villagers have undertaken a range of environmental improvements, and plan to establish the Allenheads Heritage Centre.

Energy Initiatives

Nuclear and Anti-Nuclear: There is an 'advanced' gas-cooled reactor at Hartlepool, which incorporates a 'high-tech energy information centre' — visitors are welcome with advance notice. A proposal to dump used nuclear fuel in disused chemical workings in the south of the region was dropped after massive opposition from residents and local authorities.

Druridge Bay, near Morpeth, has for some time been mooted as a possible site for a nuclear power station, and there is an active Druridge Bay Campaign to oppose the proposals. You can contact the campaign at Tower Buildings, Oldgate, Morpeth.

Alternative energy: If you are at all interested in renewable energy resources, don't miss the pioneering Northumbrian Energy Workshop, newly installed in energy-efficient premises at Acomb near Hexham. They export wind generators all over the world, and will be happy to show you their current projects and some of the excellent educational literature they produce. Langdon Common in Upper Teesdale has recently been selected by the Central Electricity Generating Board as the proposed site for an experimental 'windfarm', or group of wind generators supplying electricity to the national grid.

Of several restored watermills in the region, Tocketts Mill in Guisborough can be seen working on selected days through the summer, while Heatherslaw Mill at Etal near Berwick — England's northernmost working watermill — also has a pleasant craftshop and tearoom.

Northumbria

Transport: Train services away from the main north-south east-coast route and outside the Teesside and Tyneside conurbations are generally not particularly good; many branch lines were closed in the 1960s. Northumberland County Council produces a useful *Northumberland Public Transport Services*, while Durham (North Road) and Middlesborough (Newport Road) bus stations can provide details of local and long-distance bus services in their areas.

Bicycles are generally thin on the ground, though the local branch of the Cyclists' Touring Club (see under Newcastle) will be happy to provide information.

Food: Fish, especially herring and kippers, is a traditional mainstay of the North-East, though remember how polluted the North Sea now is. There is also a long tradition of heavy spicy cakes — singin' hinnies, spice loaf and stotty cake, all washed down with local ale (Newcastle Brown, though now a multi-national product, is a regional favourite). If you are looking for real ale, local enthusiasts produce an occasional newssheet called *Canny Bevvy*, to be found on select pub bars such as that of the Dog and Parrot near Newcastle Central Station. Leeks are a regional preoccupation, allotment growers competing to produce the most massive specimens; after September evening leek shows visitors will often be treated to a free bowl of soup.

Bookshops: The Alleycat Bookshop in New Elvet, Durham (just down from the student union, where visiting students can avail themselves of a cheap meal), is a co-operative enterprise with a good range, especially on local labour history.

Resources: See under Newcastle upon Tyne.

The North West

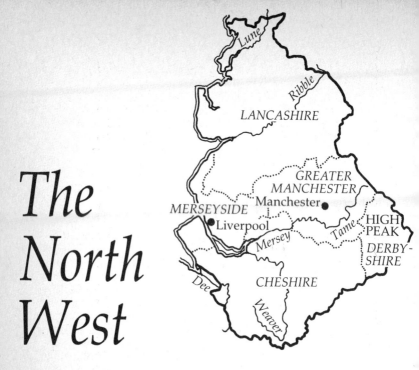

All that most travellers know about the North West is its motorway system; the North West is that long bit on the way to the Lake District and Scotland, full of drab northern towns, industrial estates and disused railway sidings. It's true that the region hit a low patch with the rapid decline in its traditional industries, but the area between the North Sea and the Pennines is worth a closer look, even if the jewels are sometimes hard to find.

North West

The North West is very much an area of mass commercially-organised fun — The Avalanche at Blackpool and Southport Pleasureland are what draw the crowds and the pennies. But this does mean less people at the really interesting places like the Trough of Bowland and Pendle Hill, Blackstone Edge and Alderley.

In the past ten years the region has suddenly become aware of its history, and 'heritage centres' like Wigan Pier and Liverpool's Albert Dock are all the vogue — if only they'd kept a bit more of the real heritage instead of knocking it down and charging people to see 'how we lived then'. Yet there is a genuine move towards community involvement in many places, and despite pockets of deprivation and poverty the North West is an exciting place to visit. Give it a chance.

MANCHESTER

Within ten miles of Manchester's imposing Town Hall live more than 2½ million people, the 'cottonopolis' which grew like Topsy between 1820 and 1910. Now ringed by boring urban motorways, its centre partially gutted by monstrosities like the Arndale Centre and the Piccadilly development, it is easy to forget that the region is still to a large extent one of urbanised villages set in the often delightful foothills of the Pennines. The rivers — the Irwell, Tame and Goyt — are still there, and an approach from the east, preferably by rail, will reveal something of the city's natural setting.

Although this entry deals specifically with the city of Manchester, the conurbation stretches north to Rochdale, the home of the co-operative movement, east to Oldham on the Pennines' edge, south towards the Peak District, and westwards beyond Salford into the Mersey plain. Many of the region's villages are well worth a visit, particularly the Pennine mill settlements, like Delph or Mossley.

North West

Manchester has a long history of radicalism, often a reaction to harsh factory conditions. 1819 was Peterloo year, a mass rebellion which did much to change industrial conditions in England; two years later the liberal campaigning newspaper *The Manchester Guardian* (now *The Guardian*) was first published. The city has a strong Jewish community, and Manchester's Chinatown is the second largest Chinese enclave in Britain.

Manchester's 'green attractions' are scattered throughout the city, so a good start is to visit the Tourist Information Centre to browse through some of the excellent material published by the City Council and the Greater Manchester Passenger Transport Executive. The free leaflet *A Stroll Round the City Centre* gives good basic information.

Tourist Information Office: Town Hall Extension, Lloyd Street (Tel: 061 234 3157/8).

Wholefood Restaurants: In the top league are On The Eighth Day at 109-111 Oxford Road (very good value) and Wild Oats at 88 Oldham Street, conveniently situated between Piccadilly and Victoria Stations. Also very central is the friendly Chaise Lounge Too at the Royal Exchange shopping precinct, while good but big and impersonal are the Farmhouse Kitchens in Fountain Street and Blackfriars Street.

Wholefood Shops: On The Eighth Day also have a very good wholefood shop at 111 Oxford Road, while the best bread (plus a good wholefood range) comes from The Green Door Bakery, a women's co-operative at 72 Hamilton Road, a bus ride north from the city centre.

Bookshops: Grass Roots at 1 Newton Street is a long-established co-operative bookshop with an extensive range and knowledgeable staff. Grass Roots stocks every local alternative publication, and displays details of upcoming events — a good place to start your exploration of grassroots Manchester.

Museums: Manchester boasts Britain's first urban heritage park at Castlefield; here you will find a reconstructed Roman fort and the impressive Urban Studies Centre. The Transport Museum houses one of the country's largest collections of public service vehicles, while the Jewish Museum, housed in the fascinating former Spanish and Portuguese Synagogue, traces the history of Britain's Jewish community.

North West

Shops and Crafts: Pedestrianised Market Street and the 1960s Arndale Centre are the ugly heart of Manchester's commercial centre; more inspiration will be found in Chinatown, between Piccadilly and Princess Street, or in the narrow Oldham and Tib Streets. Nearby you will find the Manchester Craft Village, off Oak Street, an old fishmarket converted into craft studios and stalls offering an enormous range of products from handmade dolls to glass engraving.

City Wildspaces: Not far away to east and south are the real wildspaces, but Manchester has also been at the forefront of the reclaimed wildspace movement. Between 1974 and 1982 more than 4,000 acres of industrial wasteland were reclaimed, creating ten country parks, including Moses Gate, a few minutes' walk from Farnworth town centre, and the Mersey Valley Regional Park to the south of the city. Together with the impressive eighteenth century Heaton Gardens, dramatic Boggart Hole Clough, and smaller urban parks, you are never far from greenery in most parts of the city. There are city farms at Clayton (Clague Street) and Wythenshawe (Woodhouse Lane).

Transport: Greater Manchester Passenger Transport Executive operates an extensive and efficient bus and train network; free maps and timetables are available from bus and railway stations. A light rail 'super-tram' system is planned for the city centre. Manchester still supports an extensive network of canals, and you can sample narrowboat travel on the Bridgewater, Britain's oldest canal; the Leeds and Liverpool (the country's longest) is well worth exploring — boats can be hired from several places. The Greater Manchester Cycling Project (11 Bloom Street, Manchester M1 3HS) is working to provide the city with more cycleways and safer streets. There appears to be nowhere in the city to hire bikes from.

Energy Initiatives: Watermills powered Manchester's earliest industrial revolution; an original water-powered cotton mill can be seen at Quarry Bank, Styal, ten miles south of the city centre.

Community Initiatives: The co-operative movement is strong in Manchester, as is the move towards community involvement in housing and environmental projects. Manchester Co-operative Development Agency (Holyoake House, Hanover Street, Manchester M60 0AS) will be able to tell you about the former, which cover every area of economic and cultural activity from contract cleaning to record distribution. There are several places where you can see what communities have done to look after their neighbourhoods: at Huxley Avenue in Cheetham Hill the residents' association has cleared and landscaped derelict sites; in Moss Side the ward committee has closed a sidestreet to make a playground and given a facelift to the shopfronts in Normanby Street; and at Grove Road, Stalybridge, derelict land has been turned into 'springcleaned' parkland.

Health: There is no single natural health centre in Manchester; *Cahoots* magazine contains up-to-date information about practitioners, while the Institute for Complementary Medicine Public Information number for the region is 061 766 3686.

Local Directories: An excellent introduction to green-tinted activities throughout Manchester and the North-West is *Cahoots* magazine, published bi-monthly. The listings cover everything from environmental groups to therapy and communes.

LIVERPOOL

Liverpool owes its status to the transtlantic shipping trade, and both the Victorian opulence and redbrick terraces which characterise the city are the legacy of its rapid growth in the nineteenth century. By the 1950s both had fallen out of grace with urban planners, and in the last forty years Liverpool has become the place where they keep trying again and again to build a decent cityscape, yet failing again and again because they forget to ask the people who live there what they really want. Until recently, that is. Today Liverpool — perhaps from necessity — has become a seedbed for imaginative renewal projects, community architecture, locally-based economic initiatives and urban wildspaces. Liverpool has maintained its individuality better than most English cities, which can be seen in many aspects of Scouse life, from a strong and sometimes idiosyncratic socialist local authority to the rows of books on local history and dialect in the city's bookshops.

The main dockfront has been turned into 'an attraction', its antiseptic order betraying what was once the city's heart; yards away are debris-strewn wastelands waiting for land values to rise. Much of the shopping centre west of Lime Street Station has been pedestrianised, and only the street markets prevent the area from extreme anonymity. The bold tenemented streets around the city's two

North West

cathedrals — both well worth a visit — provide walks of a more uplifting nature, while a bus ride south into Toxteth or Aigburth will give you a better idea of the real Liverpool, boarded-up 1950s flats and long low 1850s terraces alongside Victorian mansions and formal parks.

Tourist Information Offices: 29 Lime Street (Tel: 051 709 3631); Atlantic Pavilion, Albert Dock (Tel: 051 708 8854).

Wholefood Restaurants: Surprisingly, there isn't the sort of friendly scrubbed-pine co-operative restaurant you might expect to find in a city like Liverpool, though both the Everyman Bistro (attached to the Everyman Theatre) at 9-11 Hope Street and the Café Berlin at 77 Bold Street offer wholesome fare at reasonable prices. If you're near the university students' union building in Bedford Street North around lunchtime on a weekday during termtime, the Nature's Way wholefood café is open to the public and is excellent value for money.

Wholefood Shops: Liverpool is not well off for wholefood shops, and if you want a decent range you will have to make your way to the Dancing Cat co-operative at 107 Lodge Lane, not far from Edge Hill station.

Bookshops: News from Nowhere is Liverpool's radical bookshop and information place; here you will find a rack of local magazines and an excellent book selection; NfN will shortly be moving from the sad and rundown end of Whitechapel (number 100) to a bright new shop near the top of Bold Street.

Museums: The Maritime Museum at Albert Dock is well worth a visit, as is the Museum of Labour History in the old County Sessions House in William Brown Street, very close to Lime Street Station. The Open Eye Gallery at 90/92 Whitechapel is a community exhibition space, soon to move to Bold Street alongside News from Nowhere.

Shops and Crafts: Shops in Liverpool are in general unoriginal and uninspiring, though the award-winning Cavern Walks (of Beatles fame) at the back of recently-pedestrianised Lord Street are worth a wander. There is a good Third World Tradefare shop at 64 Bold Street.

City Wildspaces: Liverpool has been at the forefront of the movement to green Britain's cities, as a wander round Toxteth or St Michaels will show. These once-desperate inner city areas have benefitted enormously from projects like the Rural Preservation Society's 'greensight' scheme. Landlife, a local wildlife group, have been very active in promoting urban wildspaces like Priory Wood

North West

in St Michaels, and the Clay Banks coastal walk behind Speke Airport; the staff at Landlife (offices at the community centre in Lark Lane) are very helpful. Rice Lane City Farm in Walton Park is worth visiting. At Riverside Nurseries in Speke, trees are grown for urban wildspace projects and sold to community groups at cost.

Transport: Bus services are good and fairly cheap; the Merseytravel shops at Williamson Square and Pier Head have timetables and a cheap citywide public transport map. Local train services are also good and frequent. There appears to be nobody hiring cycles in the city these days.

Community Initiatives: Liverpool is a hotbed of small-scale community initiatives, often supported by a farsighted city administration. For co-operative housing projects, walk round the Weller Street area of Toxteth, or the imaginative building in Hesketh Street at the back of Lark Lane. Though in danger of yuppification, Lark Lane in St Michaels with its very active community centre, cafés, church-run craft and wholefood shop, and good secondhand bookshop, is a good example of how urban communities can organise themselves — given a little encouragement.

Health: Liverpool Holistic Health Centre at 70 Rodney Street (Tel: 051 708 8607 or 051 709 1122) offers a wide range of therapies in friendly surroundings.

Local Directories: A few years ago there was an *Alternative Merseyside Directory*, but it has died a death. Two free monthlies are worth picking up at Tourist Information: *What's On Merseyside* and the City Council's *City Magazine*. *Liverpool Counter-Information* will tell you what the others daren't — if you can read the minute duplicated text.

THE REST OF THE REGION

Regional Tourist Office: North West Tourist Board, The Last Drop Village, Bromley Cross, Bolton, Lancashire BL7 9PZ (Tel: 0204 59111).

Ancient Sites: Though the region has no spectacular or famous ancient sites, most prominent hilltops, especially in Cheshire, display the remains of forts: a neolithic settlement atop Alderley Edge, an iron age fort on Helsby Hill. Thirteenth century Beeston Castle on the red sandstone ridge between Crewe and Chester commands spectacular views, while the dramatic tower at Mow Cop, east of Crewe, is actually a gothic folly. Pendle Hill near Burnley is inextricably linked with the persecution of witchcraft; here in 1612 a group of local women was tried, most being found 'guilty' and summarily executed.

North West

Trees and Woodland: Oak woodland once covered the southern part of the region; today only a few steep Pennine valleys like Warburton's Wood (permit only) retain their native vegetation, though country parks like Marbury near Northwich and Eastham on the Wirral offer pleasant woodland walks. At the northern tip of Lancashire are the important nature reserves of Eaves Wood and Gait Barrows, where mixed woodland of oak, ash, lime, beech and yew thrives among fascinating limestone formations (leaflets available locally).

Wildlife: The saltmarshes and tidal flats of the region's long coastline are important feeding and roosting grounds for waders and wildfowl: 160 species have been recorded at Morecambe Bay. The reedbeds of Leighton Moss near Morecambe provide the ideal home for rare bird and plant species; a public hide has been built so fledgling birdwatchers can see what is going on. The Wildfowl Trust manages the Martin Mere reserve near Southport, and though you will see many wild species there, considerable stress is also placed on the collection of penned and pinioned waterfowl. Cheshire's meres, the result of centuries of salt extraction, provide rich and varied wildlife habitats, as at Sandbach Flashes. It is the fate of most meres to become filled with vegetation to form mosses, and the process is well displayed and described at Risley Moss reserve, looked after by Warrington New Town Corporation (leaflets and nature trail guide available from the interpretative centre at the reserve). The local nature conservation trusts, from whom further information may be obtained, are the Lancashire Trust for Nature Conservation (Cuerden Valley Park, Bamber Bridge, Preston PR5 6AX) and the Cheshire Conservation Trust (Marbury Country Park, Northwich CW9 6AT).

Protected Areas: The Arnside and Silverdale Area of Outstanding Natural Beauty at the northern end of the region extends into southern Cumbria, and similar status has been afforded to the 310 square miles of the Forest of Bowland, a fine tract of high open moorland in north-east Lancashire.

Access to the Countryside: Access is generally limited to rights of way, even in the upland areas of the region. The Forest of Bowland is notorious for its limited access, and although the situation has improved in recent years, foresters and shooters are still first priority over much of this moorland. Among the region's long-distance paths are the Ribble Way from Preston to Gisburn, and several routes in Cheshire, including the Gritstone Trail, the Mow Cop Trail, and the Sandstone Trail (guidebooks available from Cheshire County Council Countryside and Recreation Division, County Hall, Chester CH1 1SF).

North West

Organic Initiatives: The Middle Wood Centre at Wray near Lancaster is an 'energy-conscious resource centre', managing a 115-acre organic farm and 120 acres of native woodland; the visitor centre is designed to demonstrate ecologically viable lifestyles. At Ferrocrete Farm at nearby Arkholme near Carnforth, visitors (especially children) are welcome to see organic techniques in practice and to buy organic produce. Oakcroft Gardens at Cross o'the Hill, Malpas, is an organic market garden which sells produce and acts as an educational centre for a holistic approach to food and health; courses are also offered, though they tend to discourage very short stay visitors.

Local Building Traditions: In the upland areas, the traditional building material is stone; red sandstone in north and south, millstone grit in the east and white limestone in the centre. Timber and clay were also widely used, as can be seen in the delightful fifteenth century houses of Little Moreton Hall at Congleton and Rufford Old Hall near Ormskirk. Brick was first used in the sixteenth century, and became the favourite building material in much of Cheshire and Merseyside during the industrial revolution. A good cross section of regional building techniques can be seen at the Pendle Heritage Centre at Park Hill, Barrowford, near Nelson. No lover of traditional townscape should miss Chester with its unique 'rows' — covered walkways at first floor level, timber-framed Tudor houses, Georgian brick mansions and great sandstone castle.

Museums: The North West is proud of its history of industrial innovation, and its museums display much of this rich heritage. Great steam engines can be seen at Ellenroad Mill at Newhey and Queen Street cotton mill at Harle Syke, Burnley, while the Museum of Mining at Salford tells the history of the region's other great traditional industry. The Boat Museum at Ellesmere Port has the largest collection of canal boats in England, together with restored cottages and a forge.

Community Initiatives

Community Housing and Architecture: In 1888 the 'model village' of Port Sunlight was officially opened, designed to house soap industry workers in dwellings which were both convenient and pleasing to the eye; at the Port Sunlight Heritage Centre you can learn about this philanthropic project and be shown around some of the houses. Macclesfield in Cheshire can with some justification be claimed as the birthplace of community architecture in England, for it was here in 1972 that the Black Road project was established, involving three hundred households in the complete restoration of their nineteenth century terraced houses. At nearby Roan Court, an

North West

estate of new houses has been built with the same degree of 'customer participation'. A stroll round the Black Road area today reveals an obviously cared-for neighbourhood in what could so easily have become a concrete and wasteland 'comprehensive redevelopment'.

Communal Groups: Communal projects in the region include a Burnley group called People in Common who are currently renovating a mill as living and working space; visitors are sometimes welcome with advance notice; contact them at 58 Clarence Street. There is another long-established small communal group in a village near Lancaster.

Economic Initiatives

Co-operatives: Co-operative businesses are thick on the ground in this region where the co-operative movement was born — at Rochdale you can visit the Pioneers Museum, the first co-operative shop in England, opened in 1844. At Weavers' Triangle, Burnley, volunteers have renovated and revived a Victorian industrial complex straddling the Leeds and Liverpool Canal to create a fascinating local heritage centre. The North West's many co-ops include theatre groups, video makers, most of the region's best wholefood shops, and even a co-operative group of tourist guides: Lancashire Heritage Guides at 14 Aspels Nook, Penwortham, Preston PR1 9AP. The regional Co-operative Development Council can be contacted at Holyoake House, Hanover Street, Manchester M60 0AS.

Craft Workshops: There are several projects in the region where several craftspeople share premises. At Eccles Farm Craft Centre at Bispham Green near Ormskirk, a 300-year-old barn houses workshops, a craft shop, and a restaurant. Six businesses including a textile artist and a bookbinder work in the Barn Studios at Farndon in Cheshire. At Uppermill, five miles east of Oldham, the Alexandra Craft Centre houses a wide range of craft workshops, and you can buy directly from the makers, while ten people, making a range of crafts from jigsaw puzzles to jumpers, work at the Warmington Craft Workshops near Sandbach. Unusual crafts in the region include Cheshire Candle Workers at Burwardsley, nine miles south-east of Chester, and the specialist canal craft shop at Lower Park Marina, Barnoldswick, on the Leeds and Liverpool Canal.

Energy Initiatives

Nuclear and Anti-Nuclear: Heysham gas-cooled nuclear reactor on Morecambe Bay is one of the country's newest. The 'observation tower' is open to visitors every day during the summer, and you can have a guided tour if you arrange it in advance.

North West

Alternative Energy: Two working watermills in Cheshire are occasionally used for grinding corn: Nether Alderley Mill near Macclesfield, with its fascinating overshot tandem wheel, and Stretton Mill near Farndon, which also houses a watermill museum.

Transport: Both rail and bus services are good within the more built-up areas; the standard of timetables and route maps is among the best in the country. See also under Manchester and Liverpool. Canals are still an important part of the North West scene, and boats can be hired on several of them, including the Leeds and Liverpool and the Llangollen Canal, which crosses the south-west corner of Cheshire.

Health: See under Manchester and Liverpool. The Institute for Complementary Medicine information number for the region is 061 980 5919.

Food: Cakes, cheese and offal are the regional specialities. Of the former, Eccles cakes are crammed with currants, while Bury's simnel cakes with their traditional marzipan layer are delicious. Tripe is an acquired taste, while crumbly white Cheshire cheese is delicious.

Bookshops and Resources: See under Manchester and Liverpool.

Yorkshire and Humberside

Until local government reform in 1974, Yorkshire claimed an eighth of England's area and a tenth of its population. For the bulk of Yorkshire folk it still does, even though the centuries-old county has now been divided between five different administrative regions. The easiest way to think of the region geographically is as a big square with hills down both sides, a wide valley in the middle, and the sea on the right. To the west, the millstone and limestone hills of the Pennines descend in long and often complex valleys from high moorland to the fertile Vale of York. The Derwent, a fascinating river that rises only three miles from the North Sea but then heads inland for thirty miles before joing the Ouse south of York, divides the heather-clad plateau of the North York Moors from the rolling green Wolds to the south, limestone hills which culminate in the dramatic headland of Flamborough. South of the Humber estuary, the region now also includes part of what was Lincolnshire, linked with Hull by the world's longest single-span bridge.

In few places in England is relative wilderness to be found so close to heavy industrialisation and concentrations of human population. The Pennine foothills from Sheffield north to Keighley are home to three million people. These cities and towns are built on the traditional economic bases of wool, coal and metalworking; yet even the workers in the largest factories had access to the moors, and wherever you are in urban Bradford, Leeds or Huddersfield, you can usually see the hills.

People pressure is very noticeable in many of the region's wild places, too. Busloads of tourists scour the dales in search of 'James Heriot's Yorkshire', and so many walk the Pennine Way and the Lyke Wake Walk that matting and boards are needed to protect the fragile land surface. The fine limestone country round Malham is threatened by fly-by-night contractors taking stone for suburban rockeries, and local communities by second home owners who can always outbid the locals.

The urban-rural contrast is also reflected in local politics, with the countryside being ultra-conservative and the cities more or less staunchly radical. Thus heavily-populated West Yorkshire has excellent public transport and community arts programmes, while northern and eastern ruralites depend more on private enterprise, a car for each family, and security alarms.

SHEFFIELD

Straddling the hills at the confluence of the Rivers Don and Sheaf on the eastern edge of the southern Pennines,

Yorkshire and Humberside

Sheffield has always been 'steel city'. Yet despite being heavily industrialised, Sheffield is fortunate in having fingers of countryside which penetrate almost to the city's heart. A proud civic tradition has ensured that the city has always been among the first to provide its inhabitants with community facilities, from parks and allotments to art galleries and theatres.

In common with many other northern cities, and particularly since its centre was devastated during the second world war, Sheffield has undertaken a massive reconstruction programme. Some of the early developments, like the Hyde Park slab blocks east of the station, left a great deal to be desired, but in recent years a forward-looking socialist local authority has pioneered creative experiments in housing, education, urban transport, economic and community initiatives, and environmental management.

Tourist Information Office: Town Hall Extension, Union Street (Tel: 0742 734671/2).

Wholefood Restaurants: The two best places are Just Cooking at 16-18 Carver Street, and The Bay Tree, a fish and vegetarian wholefood restaurant at 119 Devonshire Street. The restaurant at the Crucible Theatre in Norfolk Street also has a good range of healthy fare.

Wholefood Shops: There isn't a good all-round wholefood shop in central Sheffield, though both Wickers at 174 Norfolk Street and The Flour Bin at 36 Exchange Street have a good range of flours, grains, pulses, dried fruits and nuts; Wickers is primarily a specialist herb shop, carrying a range of more than 200 herbs. Down to Earth at 406 Sharrowvale Road, Hunters Bar, is a real wholefood shop, carrying a wide range, including bread and organic produce.

Bookshops: Sheffield's radical bookshop is the Independent at 69 Surrey Street, with a good general range and a useful community notice board. One of the country's best secondhand bookshops for politics and current affairs is Logos Books at 77 Junction Road, Hunters Bar — well worth a detour.

Museums: Kelham Island Industrial Museum gives a graphic impression of three centuries of Sheffield industry, including workshops where craftspeople ply their trade. The Untitled Gallery in Brown Street is a lively independent gallery which concentrates on showing and working with local community talent.

Shops and Crafts: Sheffield has a lively market in the adjacent covered areas of Castle Market and Sheaf Market, open every day except Thursday and Sunday. An open air fleamarket is held on Mondays at Setts Market, next to the Sheaf Market. Two ethnic/crafty shops worth a visit are Pippy's Boutique at 41 Cambridge Street, and Andino Latin American crafts at Balm Green, Barker's Pool.

City Wildspaces: Sheffield's favourite park is Endcliffe Park at Hunters Bar; from here you can walk up past the restored Shepherd Wheel mill right up to the edge of the moors at Ringinglow. From here the Sheffield Round Walk (booklet available) continues around the southern outskirts of the city to Abbeydale, a restored industrial hamlet, the twelfth-century abbey at Beauchief, and through Graves Park to Bunting Nook. The Rivelin Valley to the west of the city is another well-used open space, with a two-mile nature trail. The city's Wildlife Group has developed a small wildlife park at William Street, while Heeley City Farm at Richards Road is one of the longest-established urban farms in England.

Transport: There are now virtually no local train services within the city, though there are excellent and cheap bus services throughout Sheffield; details from tourist information or Pond Street bus station. Sheffield City Council is good on provision for cyclists, too — a series of five free leaflets gives details of cycle routes in the city, including a number of specially-built cycleways. Nobody appears to rent bicycles in the city.

Energy Initiatives: Both Shepherd Wheel and Abbeydale Industrial Hamlet (see under 'wildspace') have restored watermills. Sheffield Solar Building Co-op (Palatine Chambers, 22 Pinstone Street), have initiated a scheme to build 13 energy-efficient houses in the Gleadless Valley to the south of the city. There are plans to build a large CHP (combined heat and power) plant in the north-east of the city to convert industrial and domestic waste into usable energy. Sheffield has recently been chosen to be Britain's pioneering 'Recycling City'; the City Council will work with environmental and recycling agencies to set up a wide range of recycling campaigns and facilities from waste paper to glass and tin cans.

Community Initiatives: There are a number of new co-operative projects in the city, including a women's printing co-op, and The Leadmill at 6-7 Leadmill Road, a lively community arts centre with a friendly little café.

Health: There is as yet no holistic health centre in Sheffield, though there are plans to start one; in the meantime phone 0742 248181 for information about practitioners in the city.

Yorkshire and Humberside

YORK

York has many attractions for both the green and the more conventional traveller, making it an almost compulsory stop on the English tourist trail. From Roman times onwards this walled city on the River Ouse has been an important urban centre, and today retains the largest medieval church and some of the most unspoilt medieval townscape in England, Stonegate and The Shambles being the best examples.

York has a great deal to offer beyond its more distant history, however; in the nineteenth century it became an important railway centre. The recently renovated station is an impressive and graceful building, while the nearby Railway Museum houses a collection tracing the social and economic importance of Britain's rail network. The Victorian era also saw the growth of the confectionery industry, founded by the Quaker Rowntree family who did (and through a charitable trust still do) much for social reform.

The university and the city's administrative function have ensured a continuous flow of creative talent through the city, reflected in a wide range of artistic and imaginative projects organised both for visitors to the city and for its resident population. Green ideas are very much to the fore, with York playing a leading role in green initiatives such as cycling campaigns and Third World aid projects.

Tourist Information Offices: De Gray Rooms, Exhibition Square (Tel: 0904 21756/7); Railway Station (Tel: 0904 643700).

Wholefood Restaurants: The two nicest places to eat in York are The Bees Knees in Millers Yard, which is a cheap and friendly wholefood café with a limited menu, and Jane's Place in the Micklegate Arts Centre. If you hang out here for any length of time you are certain to make contact with York's green scene. Kites at 13 Grape Lane and Oat Cuisine at 13a High Ousegate are both good, but more expensive and often require advance booking. The Blake Head Café (through the bookshop at 104 Micklegate) is a new and promising self-service wholefood restaurant.

Wholefood Shops: Alligator at 104 Fishergate has York's best selection, followed closely by Nutters at 95 Walmgate. For excellent wholemeal bread and bakes (and a good range of wholefoods too) the place to go is Gillygate Wholefood Bakery, alongside The Bees Knees café in Miller's Yard. York Beershop at 28 Sandringham Street (round the corner from Alligator Wholefoods) has an excellent selection of additive-free organic beers and wines, plus some very tasty farmhouse cheeses.

Bookshops: One World at 17 Goodramgate has the best selection of books on green issues, while Godfreys at 32 Stonegate and Blake Head at 104 Micklegate are worth a browse. York also has several good secondhand bookshops, as befits its bookish character — Micklegate houses a representative selection.

Museums: The Railway Museum is worth a visit, as are the Castle Museum with its Victorian street and the Jorvik Viking Centre. If you can stand the queues and the over-commercialisation of the latter, these imaginative and faithful reconstructions do bring history to life in a very immediate way.

Shops and Crafts: As you might expect from such a tourist trap, York is awash with trendy boutiques and gifte shoppes, but there are several shops worth a particular mention. Gillygate contains several interesting businesses, including the Well Workshops in Millers Yard, providing training for young disabled people; Quilter's Patch at number 82, one of the country's few specialist shops catering for this traditional artform; and Craft Basics at number 9. One World at 17 Goodramgate has an excellent selection of Third World crafts, while local crafts can be seen and bought at the Lendal Bridge Crafts Centre at 51 Skeldergate, or the Cottage Shop at 69 Walmgate. York market, open daily except Sunday, is held in Newgate.

City Wildspaces: For a city with a population of 100,000, York is remarkably open and airy. Though there are no large parks, the riverside walk through the city centre and the 2½ mile walk around the city walls high above the rooftops provide good exercise, while several of the medieval 'strays' (fingers of common grazing land reaching in towards the city centre) provide green lungs. The North York Moors National Park is less than thirty miles away; the rolling Hambledon Hills, recently designated an Area of Outstanding Natural Beauty, even nearer.

Transport: York is a very compact city, which makes walking and cycling the obvious choices. More pedestrianisation of the city centre is planned, and there is an extensive network of cycleways, including a long-distance link with Selby to the south. Bicycles can be hired from York Cycleworks at 14-16 Lawrence Street. Details of the extensive bus and minibus service can be obtained from the tourist information offices.

Health: York Alternative Medical Practice in Museum Street (Tel: 0904 52378) offers an information and counselling service, together with a wide range of therapies.

Peace: York Peace Centre at 15a Clifford Street has a shop, notice board and small library. It is also the meeting place for several green groups.

Local Directories: The One World Shop at 17 Goodramgate has produced a very useful *Green Guide to York*.

LEEDS

The River Aire, the main reason for Leeds' once-wooded site, isn't easy to find these days, tucked as it is between the railway and tall warehouses. It was wool that the city thrived on in the eighteenth and nineteenth centuries, a wealth which led to much ornate and adventurous Victorian building. Together with the surrounding industrial towns, Leeds is now the third largest city in England, supporting a wide range of urban facilities.

The post-war period saw much concrete-and-glass rebuilding, and parts of the city, especially the northern part of the centre, suffered from a surfeit of motorway madness. Large areas are still being redeveloped with a mixture of do-it-yourself hypermarkets and car parks, but Leeds also boasts one of Europe's largest pedestrian shopping precincts, and parks that any city could be proud of. The canalside walk to Kirkstall Abbey is one of the most fascinating town walks in the country, and the Brontë's Haworth with its wild moorland walks is only a dozen miles away.

Leeds Civic Trust has produced two Town Trail booklets, which provide a good introduction to the city and its history. *Walkabout* takes you around the city centre, while *Walkabout Waterfront* takes you downstream along the Aire Valley.

Tourist Information Office: 19 Wellington Street (Tel: 0532 462454/5).

Wholefood Restaurants: Leeds has a large ethnic population, reflected in the variety of wholesome eating places. Salvo's at 115 Otley Road, Headingly, is an excellent Mediterranean and Middle

East restaurant; the Mandalay at 8 Harrison Street an Indian offering a good range of vegetarian dishes. Mr Natural's Orient Express at 53 Otley Road brings you dishes from around the world, while a more homely wholefood menu will be found at Wharf Street Café, a co-operative at 17-19 Wharf Street, or the Leeds Playhouse Restaurant in Calverley Street.

Wholefood Shops: The two real wholefood shops — both co-operatives — are Beano at 36 New Briggate and Dandy at 20 Shepherd's Lane; the former has a particularly wide range.

Bookshops: Since the demise of the Corner Bookshop in 1988, Leeds has no radical bookshop. Look out for Leeds Postcards, though, Britain's leading publisher of political and topical postcards.

Museums: Armley Mills Industrial Museum was once the world's largest woollen mill; it now tells the story of the city's textile industry. Abbey House Museum, once the gateway to Kirkstall Abbey, includes a folk gallery.

Shops and Crafts: The city has several fine Victorian covered arcades; compare the nasty 1960s Empire Arcade to see what happens when money is all that counts. The Victorian City Market at the foot of Vicar Lane is one of the best surviving covered markets in England, open every day except Sundays and Wednesday afternoons. Individual shops worth a visit include Id Aromatics at 9 Boar Lane, which sells natural fragrances, and Made to Last, a women's shoemaking co-operative at 77 Raglan Road, Woodhouse Moor.

City Wildspaces: Roundhay Park in the north-east of the city is one of the largest natural parks in the country, incorporating both formal and wild gardens. Reaching westwards from the city centre along the Leeds and Liverpool Canal is the eight-mile-long Museum of Leeds Trail; the trail passes the museums mentioned above, and takes in monuments to the history of the city from the ancient abbey at Kirkstall to the bridge carrying the M62 motorway; an informative booklet is available. There is a city farm — Meanwood Valley Urban Farm — at Sugarwell Road, Meanwood, to the north of the city.

Transport: Information about the city's extensive bus and minibus network can be obtained from the Central Bus Station in St Peter's Street. Bikes can be hired from Watson Cairns at 157 Lower Briggate.

Community Initiatives: There is a strong co-operative movement in the city; as well as several of the ventures already mentioned, Leeds co-ops include the Leeds Animation Workshop, which

Yorkshire and Humberside

specialises in radical cartoon films, and the country's largest organic wine distributors, Venceremos Ltd. The latter has its premises at Beechwood College in Elmete Lane, a centre for radical and alternative groups which can supply information about many community initiatives in and around the city. The Industrial Co-Ownership Movement, established in 1971 to foster links between co-operatively run businesses, has its head office in Leeds (7/8 The Corn Exchange).

Health: Leeds Community Health Project, 19 Providence Avenue, can provide information about practitioners and health centres in the city.

Local Directories: *Leeds Other Paper*, a radical monthly, gives details of interesting forthcoming events in the city. Leeds tourist information also produces a monthly *Leeds Leisure Magazine*.

THE REST OF THE REGION

Regional Tourist Office: Yorkshire and Humberside Tourist Board, 312 Tadcaster Road, York YO2 2HF (Tel: 0904 707961).

Ancient Sites: The North York Moors display what is probably the best-preserved prehistoric landscape in England. Archaeologist Jacquetta Hawkes estimates that 'There are still ten thousand round barrows and cairns up here among the heather and coarse moorland grass, Bronze and Iron Age hut clusters, dykes and defences of all kinds, standing stones and stone circles, long barrows.' One such standing stone is Wade's Stone, beside the road from Whitby to Loftus — tradition says it marked a giant's grave; archaeologists showed it to be that of an Anglian warrior. The nearby Roman causeway was supposed to have been built so that Wade's equally enormous wife could cross the moors to milk her mammoth cow. Not far from Wold Newton in north Humberside is the immense round barrow of Willy Howe. It stands in the usually-dry watercourse of the Gypsey Race, the appearance of which after wet weather is said to prophesy disaster.

Trees and Woodland: Little of the region's native woodland remains, though rich ash woods can still be seen at reserves like Grass Wood in Wharfedale (permit only). Most forest in the region, and most of that is in the North York Moors, is planted conifer; only drastic action by the national park authority has prevented the dark trees spreading throughout the plateau. In recent years the Forestry Commission has begun to open its Yorkshire forests to the public, and Dalby and Wykeham Forests now have nature trails and picnic areas.

Yorkshire and Humberside

Wildlife: Though the popular evocation of Yorkshire is of dark satanic mills, in fact the vast majority of the county is a combination of moorland plateau and lowland agriculture, each with its distinctive associated wildlife. Much of the upland has been overgrazed until it is a virtual desert, but in some areas, especially where the fascinating limestone landscape of the Yorkshire Dales has been preserved, there is a rich variety of flowers and grasses. In some places buzzard, peregrine and merlin still breed. In the lowlands there is less room for wildlife, though otters still breed in the upper reaches of the Derwent, and Wheldrake Ings near York (permit only) is an internationally important wetland site, where thousands of wildfowl overwinter each year. Many of the nature reserves in the region are administered by the Yorkshire Wildlife Trust, 10 Toft Green, York YO1 1JT.

Protected Areas: Yorkshire and Humberside is the only English tourist board region to cover three of England's ten national parks. In fact only the edge of the Peak District park (see the 'Shires' chapter) is in the region, but all of the North York Moors and nearly all of the Yorkshire Dales fall within it.

The Yorkshire Dales National Park is a vast limestone area, rising to the dramatic millstone-capped peaks of Ingleborough, Whernside and Penyghent. More than two hundred miles of underground passage lie under the strange 'clint and grike' (limestone pavement and the cracks therein) landscape, while the much-studied and much-visited Malham Tarn is an unparalleled wetland limestone site. Nearby is Gordale Beck, which plunges over a sixty-foot scar to form what is probably the finest limestone waterfall in the country.

The North York Moors National Park is one of England's largest expanses of heather moor, underlain for the most part by acid sandstone. The fringing woodlands contain a great variety of plants, including rare orchids, while Farndale is famed for its wild daffodils (though it is hard to avoid the crowds here in springtime). Parts of the coast are quite spectacular, rivalling the Dorset coast for interest and exhilaration. Much of this coastline, together with the area around Flamborough Head, has been designated a heritage coast.

Access to the Countryside: In the upland areas, access is not generally a problem, though the Ministry of Defence land at Fylingdales in the North York Moors is inaccessible, and wet marshland can defy the most intrepid wanderer. In the lowlands, the rights of way system is reaonably comprehensive and well-signed, especially near the cities. The long-distance Pennine Way crosses the west of the region, while the Wolds Way and Cleveland Way link up at Filey to provide a long-distance walking route from

Yorkshire and Humberside

Hull to Redcar, then around the northern and western flanks of the North York Moors to Helmsley. Guidebooks are available for all these paths. Other long-distance paths include the famous Lyke Wake Path across the North York Moors (guidebook available); the Ebor Way from Helmsley to Ilkley via York; and the Colne Valley Circular Walk which starts in Huddersfield (booklets from the Colne Valley Society, 58 Pennine View, Linthwaite, Huddersfield HD7 5SD).

Organic Initiatives: Probably the most interesting organic initiative in Yorkshire is Ridgeway Organic Farm (Kent House, Ridgeway, Sheffield 12), seven miles south of Sheffield, which doubles as a co-operative organic education centre and commercial fruit and vegetable farm. Other organic farms in the region selling produce include Church House fruit farm at Scackleton, Hovingham, near York, and Bracken Farm at Priestly Green, Norwood Green, near Halifax, where they grow a range of vegetables and bush fruit.

Local Building Traditions: Solid stone houses with small windows to keep out the wet are the hallmark of Yorkshire architecture, though local stone has always been used on a grander and more decorative scale, too: witness the grandeur of York Minster, built from the Triassic limestone which underlies the Vale of York. In the textile areas of West Yorkshire you can still see what architectural historian Nikolaus Pevsner called 'Halifax houses', the yeoman clothiers' dwellings with long rows of mullioned windows, and weavers' cottages with rows of windows under the eaves to lighten the loom-chamber. Medieval buildings survive in York, though timbered buildings are now scarce in West Yorkshire — Lambert's Arcade in Leeds contains one of that city's few survivors. Brick took over from stone in the central lowlands during the nineteenth century, and the hallmark of the suburbs of cities like York and Doncaster is long terraces of red brick, often with the local limestone used to provide a touch of decoration, even on the humblest houses.

Museums: Worth going a long way to see, Halifax's Piece Hall is an imaginative conversion of the massive eighteenth-century building where wool traders once displayed their wares. It now houses displays about every aspect of the history of Calderdale, with regular demonstrations and hands-on exhibits.

Community Initiatives

Communal Groups: At Townhead, Dunford Bridge, on the edge of the Peak District between Sheffield and Huddersfield, is the Lifespan community, a living and working co-operative which has renovated two terraces of cottages and currently houses twelve

Yorkshire and Humberside

people. Their main source of income is their own printing and publishing business, based on the premises. Visitors, especially if you want to stay a few days and join in with whatever needs doing, are welcome — but only with advance notice.

Economic Initiatives

Co-operatives: Apart from the cities already covered, the co-operative movement in Yorkshire is by far the strongest in the west of the region. Suma Wholefoods at Dean Clough Industrial Park in Halifax were one of the first wholefood wholesalers in England, and are still the largest; interested visitors are welcome with advance notice. Dean Clough, originally a massive carpet factory, has in the last five years been transformed into a network of small community businesses, which between them now employ over 1,800 people, giving the town of Halifax a new sense of economic direction. As well as manufacturing and wholesaling firms, Dean Clough houses an art gallery, a theatre, an innovation centre, a small business advice centre, a restaurant and a pub. If you are particularly interested in wholefoods, you may also like to know about Food and Futures in Todmorden (49 Halifax Road; technically just over the boundary into Lancashire), who provide research and ancillary services to wholefood shops throughout the country.

Craft Workshops: Though the region is home to a wide range of craft industries, woodworking is what Yorkshire is best known for. The Thirsk area in North Yorkshire is the main centre, where at several workshops like Robert Thompson's at Kilburn you can see native seasoned oak being worked by hand into fine furniture. At Holme-upon-Spalding-Moor near Market Weighton is The Rocking Horse Shop, where new horses are made and old ones renovated, and at Hebden Bridge is Walkley's, England's only complete surviving clog mill. Grewelthorpe near Ripon is the home of Grewelthorpe Handweavers, where a range of English elm hand looms is for sale as well as cloth and clothing, while at Valley House Craft Studio at Ruston near Scarborough you can try your hand at lace making and bobbin-making — or you can just buy.

Energy Initiatives

Nuclear and Anti-Nuclear: There are no nuclear power stations in the region, though the Drax and Ferrybridge conventional coal-fired stations, well-known landmarks to all users of the main A1 route into south Yorkshire, are England's largest and dirtiest. A belated scheme to clean up their poisonous sulphur discharges is now under way. Nuclear dumping is a threat to Humberside; Humberside Against Nuclear Dumping can be contacted at 3 Thorngarth Lane, Barrow-on-Humber. There is a more-or-less

Yorkshire and Humberside

permanent peace camp outside the US nuclear spy base at Menwith near Harrogate; the contact number for the support group is 0532 576569.

Alternative Energy: Wind in the east and water in the west helped to fuel Yorkshire's agriculture and industry, though few of these mills are working today. You can see a working windmill at Skidby, near Beverley, while the Leeds Industrial Museum and the Shepherd Wheel in Sheffield show different scales of watermill. Just south of Boroughbridge, beside the road to York, you can see a recently-erected 100 kilowatt windmill, looking very graceful in its wooded hilltop setting.

Transport: British Rail's Yorkshire network is based on Leeds, from where lines with traditional regional names radiate westwards into the Dales and east towards York and Darlington. Within West Yorkshire, trains and buses are reasonably well integrated, and special fare passes can be used on both. Bus services, good near the cities but hardly existent in many rural areas, are run by a variety of companies, the main ones including West Yorkshire (East Parade, Harrogate: for the north-west of the region) and East Yorkshire (Ferensway Coach Station, Hull: for the south-east). While the upland areas are more suitable for walking than cycling, the Wolds and the Vale of York are ideal for bicycles; see under York for cycle hire.

Health: See under Leeds, Sheffield and York. The Institute for Complementary Medicine local information service number is 027 458 6708.

Food: The world-famous Yorkshire pudding is not to be missed, and is increasingly offered as it was originally intended, as a course in its own right with a rich onion gravy. Parkin, a rich treacly cake, is the other well-known speciality.

Bookshops: See under Sheffield and York.

Heart of England

It is said — and can be imagined, even if not the literal truth — that from the ridge of the Malvern Hills you can on a clear day see a fifth of the area of England. Flanked by the relatively high land of Wales, the Pennines and the Chiltern escarpment, and drained by the country's longest rivers, this region covers an enormous area of lowland England. In the east it merges imperceptibly with the shires of Leicester and Northampton, but in the north-

Heart of England

west and south-west the lines of communication narrow towards Crewe and Bristol.

Yet the Heart of England is by no means flat, as the distinctive shapes of the Shropshire hills and the Malverns testify. Even the area around Birmingham is hilly, necessitating numerous railway and canal tunnels. Though every region claims diversity and contrast, this is more true of the Heart of England than of any other. To walk the canalside under Gravelly Hill's 'spaghetti junction' is to experience the worst that pollution and concrete can do to the earth. To climb Titterstone Clee on a warm spring day is to renew your faith in natural beauty.

Much of what in the coal era was dubbed The Black Country remains sad and derelict in the aftermath of Birmingham's first industrial boom; some is coming to life again in the redbrick and plastic facelift of the city's newfound importance as the distribution centre for materialist England. In many places the green belt is struggling against housing estates and out-of-town shopping centres, though some derelict sites are now receiving a new lease of life as urban wildspaces, and parts of the conurbation retain much of their small-scale village character.

Away from the built-up West Midlands, the region soon reverts to something of its rural peace, and by the time you reach the villages of the Cotswolds, the lanes of the Wye Valley, or the path along Wenlock Edge, you can for a while forget the motorways and neon-lit concrete precincts. The threats to this serenity are ever-present — Shropshire has lost nearly two-thirds of its ancient woodland in the last fifty years, and five times as many sheep graze the Long Mynd as are healthy for its heather moorland — yet green initiatives are conspicuous in many places, and it is interesting that nearly all of the Green Party's successes in local elections have been in this region.

BIRMINGHAM

'The Big Heart of England' they say of Birmingham, accompanied in the advertisements by big red hearts. Big it certainly is, and when approaching the city by train or bus, especially on a wet day, you may understand why Queen Victoria chose to pull down the blinds of her carriage rather than see what the Black Country had to offer. The heart of the city, like that of nearby Coventry, was heavily bombed in 1940. Much of the postwar rebuilding was disastrous — the worst of mass concrete municipal and anonymous elevated roadway. Twenty-five years of weathering and grafitti have only for the most part made things worse.

So what does Birmingham have going for it? To begin with there is, luckily, far more to Birmingham than its city centre. Less than half a mile from the hideous twins of the Bullring Centre and New Street Station you can be in the relative sanity of Allison Street (the centre of Birmingham's green activism) or Gas Street Basin, a busy and colourful canal junction. A short bus ride will bring you to Birmingham's Nature Centre or to Moseley Bog, a Site of Special Scientific Interest and the inspiration for Tolkein's River Withywindle.

While the university suburb of Edgbaston retains much of its Victorian charm and house prices to match, the northern outskirts, home to a racial mix found in few parts of England, are also the proving grounds for a range of community initiatives. Ashram Acres in Sparkbrook is a thriving enterprise using wasteland to produce European and Asian vegetables, while in nearby Walsall waste segregation and recycling provides an income for local charities, and community associations like that at The Pleck provide real hope for disadvantaged areas.

Tourist Information Office: 2 City Arcade (Tel: 021 780 4321).

Wholefood Restaurants: There is nothing very good very central; the best eating places are ranged in a semicircle, from west to south and a couple of miles out. Nutters at 422 Bearwood Road,

Heart of England

Bearwood, is good and cheap; La Santé an upmarket French vegetarian at 182-184 High Street, Harborne; Wild Oats a small, friendly, long-established and award-winning restaurant at 5 Raddlebarn Road, Selly Oak; and Gingers at 7a High Street, King's Heath, a student favourite offering international vegetarian specialities.

Wholefood Shops: The One Earth Shop (see 'shops and crafts'), sells some wholefoods, but for a full range you will need to go to Food for Thought at Martineau Square, or Natural World at 566 Bearwood Road, Smethwick.

Bookshops: Key Books at 136 Digbeth is Birmingham's radical bookshop, with a wide range of books on political and environmental topics. The One Earth Shop has some green titles.

Museums: Of several rather unimaginative museums, the most worthwhile are the Birmingham Railway Museum in Tyseley, and the Bus and Transport Museum in Wythall — there is a special bus service linking the two. The city's Art Gallery in Colmore Row has a fine collection of pre-Raphaelite paintings, including several by Birmingham-born Edward Burne-Jones.

Shops and Crafts: Birmingham city centre is a tiring place to shop in, with a passé fifties feel and far too much concrete and stale air. One redeeming feature is the open air 'rag market' around St Martin's Parish Church — the produce market can be found in the bowels of the Bull Ring Centre. Don't miss the One Earth Shop at 54 Allison Street, Digbeth, a small shop but with a reasonable range of organic veggies, wholefoods, books and recycled stationery — a good source of citywide green information, too.

City Wildspaces: West Midlands urban wildlife campaigners have been incredibly active for the last eight years, and Birmingham has a conservation strategy and projects on the ground that should be the envy of other English cities. As well as Moseley Bog, you can visit more than three dozen designated and managed wildspaces within the metropolitan county. One of the most imaginative is at the Ackers, not far from the Railway Museum, where forty-five acres of derelict land have been reclaimed as a wildlife garden; atop a small artificial hill is a direction-finder giving information about what can be seen all around. Birmingham has more canals than Venice, and canal towpaths, often newly restored, provide interesting walking away from the ubiquitous traffic. There are city farms at Hawbush Urban Farm in Brierley Hill and Woodgate Valley City Farm in Harborne.

Birmingham is the home of the co-ordinating organisation Think Green (Premier House, 43-48 New Street) which campaigns nationwide for greener cities: South Aston Community Park (Upper Sutton Street) is a good example of projects they have sponsored.

Transport: Local train and bus services are generally good and well co-ordinated; West Midlands Travel produces a clear and useful route map, available from the Travel Shop at 114 Colmore Row. Birmingham is very keen on cycling, with an active local campaigning group called Pushbikes supported by a sympathetic local authority. *Cycling in Birmingham*, a £2.95 book available from tourist information, tells you absolutely everything you need to know about cycling in the city, together with detailed route maps. Cycles can be hired from Tower Cycles, 172-178 Gravelly Lane, Erdington, and Harborne Cycle Surgery, 60 Wood Lane, Harborne.

Energy Initiatives: At Tyseley, again not far from the Railway Museum, is one of the country's first 'warmth from waste' incinerators, producing electricity from domestic and industrial rubbish rather than putting it in holes in the ground and hoping it will go away; a second such scheme is planned for the Wolverhampton incinerator.

Community Initiatives: The three projects mentioned in the introduction are visitable with advance notice: Ashram Acres, 23-25 Grantham Road, Sparkbrook; Walsall Area Recycling (affectionately known as the Walsall Wombles), 47 Bath Street, Walsall; and The Pleck Community Co-operative, Mountrath Street, Walsall. At Gerrard Street in Lozells, a former Methodist church has been transformed into a community music workshop, with studios and meeting rooms, while another community project has given a facelift to Smethwick High Street — the mosaics decorating several of the shopfronts were created by local children. There are many similar projects within the city; you can find out more from Community Networks Inner City Unit, 168 Corporation Street, or from Birmingham Co-operative Development Agency, 3rd Floor, Bridge House, Bull Ring Centre, Smallbrook Queensway. The New University (24 South Road, Hockley) organises various events on green themes, and has initiated an organic allotment scheme; the organisers appreciate visits from anyone involved in similar educational projects.

Health: Birmingham Centre for Alternative Medicine offers a wide range of therapies and counselling at 5 Arthur Road, Edgbaston (Tel: 021 454 7420).

Local Directories: The fortnightly free magazine *What's On* will keep you informed of current happenings, especially in the arts. Birmingham Friends of the Earth, based in Allison Street, produce a useful bi-monthly *Action Briefing: Birmingham Environmental News*, obtainable from the One Earth Shop, and the West Midlands Environment Network (3 Tower Street, Birmingham B19 3RL) have a very good monthly newsletter called *Talking Green*, which lists forthcoming events and includes information about a wide range of green initiatives.

THE REST OF THE REGION

Regional Tourist Office: Heart of England Tourist Board, 2-4 Trinity Street, Worcester WR1 2PW (Tel: 0905 613132).

Ancient Sites: Hardly a prominent hill in the west of the region is without the remains of an Iron Age fort, hardly a Cotswold parish without its barrows — stone burial chambers topped with an earthen mound. Then, in the eighth century, the Mercian King Offa ordered the building of the great earthwork between England and Wales that now bears his name. The Offa's Dyke Path now runs from Prestatyn in the north to Chepstow in the south, the best stretch of the dyke being at Rushock Hill between Kington and Knighton in Herefordshire. Legends about giants abound — The Wrekin, a steep-sided hill which is a landmark throughout north Shropshire, is said to have been deposited there by a stupid giant who intended his spadeful for the fledgling town of Shrewsbury. Osebury Rock, a headland overlooking the River Teme near Lulsley in Worcestershire, is a traditional haunt of the fairies, while Blake Mere near Leek in Staffordshire has had a reputation for mermaids and boggarts since at least the twelfth century.

Trees and Woodland: As the combined result of felling and Dutch elm disease, the region lost a third of its broadleaf woodland between 1947 and 1982, a larger proportion than any other part of England. The decline has been particularly marked in the east; much of Warwickshire has been transformed, while large areas of Shropshire and Herefordshire have changed very little. Of the two great medieval forests of the region, Shakespeare's Arden is hardly traceable save in pockets like Crackley Wood near Kenilworth (nature trail, leaflet). The great Forest of Dean, England's most unspoilt industrial area, is still largely intact, with an extensive network of woodland trails, details of which can be obtained from the Dean Heritage Centre at Camp Mill, near Cinderford.

Wildlife: Both the intensively-farmed arable lands of Warwickshire and the West Midlands metropolis leave little space for wildlife, though it is fascinating to see nature's bounty wherever land is managed on an ecological basis. At Draycote Meadows near Rugby (permit only) you can still see green-winged orchid, yellow rattle and cowslips; the abandoned gravelpits of Brandon Marsh near Coventry (permit only) provides an important stopover for

Heart of England

migrant birds. At the wilder fringes of the region, wildlife is more abundant and less threatened, though there are areas of poorer land near to centres of population which by accident of history and industry have been left relatively untouched. Such is Cannock Chase, a large area of heathland in southern Staffordshire, where a reduction in grazing is encouraging the recolonisation of native woodland species and their attendant wildlife. Perhaps the most surprising wild species in the region is the wallabies of north-east Staffordshire, the remnants of a group that escaped from a private collection during the war. If you are interested in birds, Slimbridge Wildfowl Sanctuary on the south bank of the Severn in Gloucestershire is home to a spectacular array of duck, swans, geese and waders, especially during the winter migrations; Slimbridge is also the national headquarters of The Wildfowl Trust. For more information about wildlife in the region, the local conservation trusts are: Shropshire Trust for Nature Conservation (Agriculture House, Barker Street, Shrewsbury SY1 1QP); Staffordshire NCT (Courts House, Sandon ST18 0DN); Warwickshire NCT (1 Northgate Street, Warwick CV34 4SP); Herefordshire NT (25 Castle Street, Hereford HR1 2NW; Worcestershire NCT (Hanbury Road, Droitwich WR9 7DO); and Gloucestershire TNC (Church House, Standish, Stonehouse GL10 3EU).

Protected Areas: The far north-east corner of the region falls within the Peak District national park (see the 'Shires' chapter for more information). As well as Cannock Chase, there are four other designated Areas of Outstanding Natural Beauty: the Cotswold Hills of Gloucestershire, the Shropshire Hills, the Malvern Hills, and the Wye Valley.

Access to the Countryside: In the heavily populated areas, access is limited strictly to public rights of way, and you may well find many of these ploughed up or otherwise inaccessible. The open uplands of the Malverns, the Shropshire Hills and the White Peak offer more choice, and especially near built-up areas, many signposted nature trails have been established in recent years. As well as the Offa's Dyke Way (see under 'ancient sites'), long-distance paths in the region include the 100-mile long Cotswold Way (various guides available), the Wychavon Way from the River Severn to the Cotswolds (leaflet from Wychavon District Council, Norbury House, Friar Street, Droitwich WR9 8EG), and the Staffordshire Way (two booklets from Staffordshire County Council Planning Department, Martin Street, Stafford ST16 2LE).

Organic Initiatives: The flagship of the English organic movement is undoubtedly the National Centre for Organic Gardening at Ryton-on-Dunsmore near Coventry, where you can see demon-

Heart of England

stration gardens including a wildlife garden, buy seeds, equipment and books from the shop, and eat in the excellent restaurant. At 49 Gravel Hill, Ludlow, is the Holmleigh Centre for Living Foods, an educational centre for healthy organic nutrition, while Fordhall Farm near Market Drayton in Shropshire produces a wide range of organic foods, which together with a small café in summer makes a worthwhile visit. Willows Nurseries at Newtown Lane, Leominster, grow a range of fruit and vegetable using the ecological principles of permaculture, and Green Acres at Dinmore near Hereford is an all-organic fruit farm.

Land and Agriculture: Cotswold Farm Park at Guiting Power near Cheltenham is the centre for the Rare Breeds Survival Trust, and has the most comprehensive collection of rare British domestic breeds in the country. There are also farm trails, a shop and a friendly restaurant. Acton Scott Working Farm Museum near Church Stretton is designed to show what farm life was like before petrol and electricity; traditional crafts are still plied, and there is much that a modern farmer could learn from these age-old techniques. The fact that English farmers are becoming more involved with green issues is demonstrated at a mixed farm called The Leen, just north of Pembridge in Herefordshire, where a courageous farmer has planted trees and encouraged wildlife, giving over a tenth of the area to conservation; this is not an organic farm, but at least nature gets a chance.

Local Building Traditions: While Birmingham and Coventry retain relatively little of traditional architectural merit, there is probably more of England's built heritage surviving in the rural parts of this region than anywhere else in the country. You can see exquisite Elizabethan brick, timber and plaster manor houses at Upton Cressett and Stokesay in Shropshire, the fifteenth century tithe barn at Ashleworth near Gloucester, and townscapes like those of Shrewsbury and Gloucester which have few equals in the country — the buildings housing the Gloucester Folk Museum in Westgate Street are a typical assemblage of Tudor and Jacobean half-timbered town dwellings.

Museums: The National Waterways Museum is an interesting canal collection housed in a restored Gloucester warehouse, and around Ironbridge in Shropshire is an impressive array of industrial museums centred on the world's first cast iron bridge — it gets very busy in summer, however. On a lighter note, the Napton Nickelodeon (Napton-on-the-Hill, Warwickshire) has an outstanding collection of mechanical musical instruments, right up to a pair of 1930s theatre organs.

Heart of England

Community Initiatives

Community Housing and Architecture: The Wellington area of northern Shropshire was designated the New Town of Telford in 1968, and in recent years several experimental housing schemes have been launched, including the Lightmoor Housing Project, a self-build scheme sponsored by the Town and Country Planning Association. So far fourteen houses are being built to create a small village community, though land is available for up to five hundred households. Interested visitors are welcome with advance warning, especially those with building skills; the address is Lightmoor Community Association, The Poplars, Lightmoor Road, Telford.

Communal Groups: This is very much a region of communal initiatives, and with advance notice visitors are usually welcome at a number of them. At Storridge near Malvern is Birchwood Hall, a rural group of twelve adults and six children, while Canon Frome Court near Ledbury is a large well-established community of fifty people living semi-communally. Crabapple community at Berrington Hall near Shrewsbury is a rural income-sharing group which among other things runs Crabapple Wholefoods in Shrewsbury, the town's best wholefood shop. Alongside the Benedictine Prinknash Abbey in Gloucestershire is Taena, a six-family community on a medium-sized dairy farm, with particular interests in pacifism and self-exploration — their address is Whitley Court, Upton St Leonards, Gloucester.

Economic Initiatives

Co-operatives: Outside the West Midlands metropolitan area, there are not as yet very many co-operatives in the region, and most of these are involved in the things you might expect, like wholefoods and bookselling.

Craft Workshops: Of many craft centres, the most interesting include the Cirencester Workshops, seventeen craft businesses sharing a converted brewery in this attractive Cotswold town, and the St Julian's Craft Centre in Shrewsbury, where ten businesses from shoemaking to pottery share a renovated medieval church. Hatton Craft Centre, three miles north of Warwick, and Jinney Ring Craft Centre at Hanbury near Bromsgrove are both award-winning conversions of old buildings which house a wide array of craft industries. At Cotswold Woollen Weavers near Lechlade in Gloucestershire is a display of Cotswold wool-working and a pleasant shop, and Black Sheep have a shop selling natural oiled wool garments at 39 Sheep Street, Stratford-upon-Avon.

Heart of England

Energy Initiatives

Nuclear and Anti-Nuclear: Berkeley Nuclear Power Station, on the banks of the Severn estuary, has the dubious distinction of being the world's first commercial nuclear plant; visitors are welcome with prior notice. Birmingham Friends of the Earth at 54 Allison Street will be able to give you details of anti-nuclear activities in the region.

Alternative Energy: Chadwell Mill near Newport in Shropshire has been fully restored; you can buy flour and afternoon tea in the adjacent building.

Transport: This large region is served by such a vast number of public transport operators that it would be tedious to list them — bus and rail stations and tourist information offices should be able to give you the information you need. For cyclists, the regional tourist board has produced an excellent information leaflet called *Cycling in the Heart of England*, while British Rail encourages cyclists to use their Stratford line with a useful leaflet entitled *Cycling in the Shakespeare Country*.

Health: See under Birmingham. There are also natural health centres offering a range of therapies in Oswestry (Centre of Natural Health Therapy, 22 Upper Brook Street; Tel: 0691 656331); Tamworth (Tamworth Alternative Therapy Centre, Lower Gungate Street; Tel: 0827 68374); and Hereford (Hereford Natural Health Centre, 16 Bridge Street; Tel: 0432 279653).

Food: The regional tourist board produces the useful *Food and Drink: A Taste of the Heart of England*, concentrating on the regional specialities of cider, beer and fruit-growing. Hereford is the cider capital, where you can visit the Museum of Cider in Whitecross Road. Both Bass and Burton Beers have brewing museums at Burton on Trent in Staffordshire. During the fruit-picking season you will find it hard to ignore the many roadside stands displaying the local harvest for sale.

Local Resources: *Green Drum* is a Birmingham-based quarterly; the latest issue will tell you what green events are planned in the region. Gloucestershire has a very good 'green yearbook' called *The Gloucestershire Directory*; its organisers also run an alternative information centre in Cheltenham (Tel: 0242 574795).

Bookshops: Coventry's Wedge Bookshop at 13 High Street has an excellent selection of green and radical titles, and also has a wholefood café. Cactus Community Bookshop in Stoke-on-Trent (3 Howard Place, Shelton) is also a centre for information about interesting developments in the Stoke area.

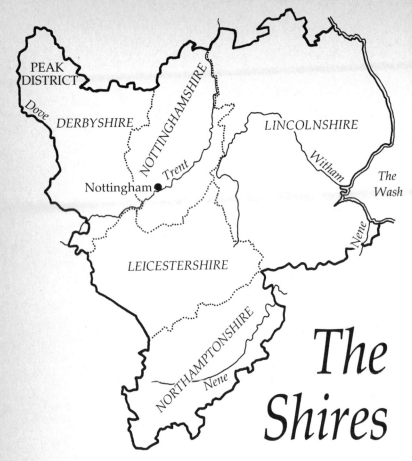

The Shires

The Shires of middle England, also known prosaically as the East Midlands, is for its size the least visited of England's regions. This is partly that there are, Matlock Baths and Sherwood Forest apart, few 'tourist attractions' in the region that many people have heard of; one of the most widely-used American guides to Britain ignores the area completely, giving no mention at all to cities like Leicester and Nottingham.

The appeal of rural East Midlands can verge on the melancholic: 'utterly still days when the sky seems to press down on an empty countryside,' writes historian W.G. Hoskins, 'when the water in the old canals lies leaf-strewn and idle, and the bridle-paths go gently on for

The Shires

mile after mile with no one in sight, past the dark spinneys, the ash-trees and the lonely spires.' Yet much of this rich agricultural landscape is alive with development talk — building land near towns with stations feeding London is at a great premium, rolling Belvoir Vale is to be the site of Britain's largest opencast coal mine, intensive farming creates barley barons alongside bankruptcy, and beautiful villages become the understandable targets of second-home owners — two nations within one village.

The red-brick cities of the region, built on textiles, steel and bureaucracy, teeter between staid conservatism and radical socialism, the latter now winning by a short head. Proud civic traditions built town halls, galleries and concert halls, laid out parks and municipal gardens; the needs of low-paid factory work and relatively cheap housing have attracted an ethnic mix rarely found outside England's big metropolises.

Though Northamptonshire and Lincolnshire are crossed by the northern extension of the limestone hills which further south form the Cotswold escarpment, the region's only real hills are in the north-west, where Derbyshire includes most of the Peak District National Park. This relatively small area attracts millions of day trippers from the surrounding cities; more people visit the narrow defile of Dovedale in a year than visit the whole of the Northumberland National Park. Meadow flowers were being trampled to extinction, litter becoming a nightmare, until cars were removed from the valley and the footpath system completely rebuilt.

Dovedale is in danger of becoming a victim of its own popularity, but if you can live without seeing Dove Holes and Tissington Spires, Lover's Leap and a thousand other visitors, the Shires have hundreds of miles of footpath where you can walk all day and see only a handful of other people. And in this region proud of its homely fare, you will almost certainly find a pub at lunchtime for a Stilton ploughman's and a glass of local ale. What more could the discerning traveller ask for?

NOTTINGHAM

Snotingaham was founded by the Danes in the ninth century, but it rose to prominence in the nineteenth, largely thanks to the foresight and talent of three rags-to-riches industrialists who also became considerable benefactors to their native city. One, Frank Bowden of Raleigh Street, founded his cycle business in 1887; Raleigh now build a million and a quarter bikes every year and ship them to every corner of the globe. While the other two — Jesse Boot (of Boots the Chemists) and John Player (of the cigarettes) — may in green terms have done a great deal less for life on earth, they are all representative of the innovative free-thinking spirit that has always characterised 'The Queen of the Midlands'.

When the new Town Hall and Council House Arcade were opened in the Old Market Square in 1929, it looked as though Nottingham was destined for another era of proud civic architecture and planning. The post-war development boom soon put an end to that aspiration. Market Sqare became 'Slab Square' (its market transferred to the anonymous covered building in Glasshouse Street), the ugly ring road (quaintly named Maid Marian Way) was cut through the medieval streets near the castle, the concrete bulk of the Broad Marsh Centre lopped off the organic curve of Listergate, and the massive Victoria Shopping Centre was only redeemed by the clocktower of the old station and Rowland Emmett's ingenious waterclock.

Nottingham now seems to have learned from its mistakes, and is pioneering urban pedestrianisation, public transport and cycleways. Always a liberal-minded city, Nottingham has also led the way in community education, trades-unionism, and initiatives to combat discrimination. England's first race relations officer was appointed here in 1958, the city was the first to provide Braille direction finders in shopping streets, and women have played an important part in Nottingham's politics

The Shires

for over a century.

The historian A.L. Rowse described Nottingham as 'a magnificent city, full of improbable splendours.' Some are more apparent than others, but whatever your green-tinted interest, the city is worth a second look.

Tourist Information Office: 16 Wheeler Gate (Tel: 0602 470661).

Wholefood Restaurants: Near the centre you have the choice of Ten at 10 Commerce Square, High Pavement, or Maxine's Salad Table at 56 Upper Parliament Street near the Theatre Royal. If you're on the north side of town or prepared to take a short walk, Veggies at 180 Mansfield Road is a co-operative producing vegan dishes to take away and displaying information about a range of green issues.

Wholefood Shops: Of a number of shops in the city selling wholefoods, the two to make for are Ouroboros at 37a Mansfield Road, one of the original co-operatives and as sound as they come, and Hiziki, a more recently-founded co-operative at 15 Goosegate.

Bookshops: Nearly all the big bookshop chains have made it to Nottingham, but an early co-operative and by far the best place for stimulating books is Mushroom at 10-12 Heathcote Street. The noticeboard at Mushroom is a good place to find out the what and where of important things going on in the city.

Museums: Of Nottingham's eight municipal museums (admission to them all is free, except to the Castle and Wollaton Hall on Sundays), there are three of special interest to the green-at-heart. The Industrial Museum, housed in the old stables at Wollaton Park, recollects the city's technological past; the Canal Museum near the railway station brings this neglected form of transport to life; and at Green's Mill, a short bus ride along Southwell Road from the city centre, a museum about windmills has been constructed around the restored windmill designed by the renowned nineteenth-century mathematician George Green.

Shops and Crafts: The city's main market is held daily adjacent to the Victoria Shopping Centre, while on Monday and Saturday mornings the Sneinton craft and bric-a-brac market can be found in Bath Street. Bridlesmith Gate and Hockley are good for interesting little shops, and for Third World crafts it is worth making the effort to get to Ujamaa, a co-operative at 14 Radford Road. In general, however, Nottingham's shopping streets tend to be boringly cosmopolitan and very crowded — Clumber Street is said to be the busiest pedestrian street in Europe.

The Shires

City Wildspaces: For relative peace close to the city centre, the Canal Walkway or the banks of the Trent provide the best walks. A little further east are Colwick Park and the country park at Holme Pierrepont, though in summer they are noted more for their human activity than for their wildlife. In the winter, however, both offer sanctuary to impressive numbers of waterfowl. Four miles north of the city is Bestwood Country Park, again full of people on summer Sundays, but large enough to lose yourself in. Nottingham's city farm is Bulwell Urban Farm, on Crabtree Farms Estate to the north-west of the city.

Transport: Both Nottingham City Transport, Lower Parliament Street (for city buses) and Trent Buses, Victoria Bus Station (for Nottinghamshire beyond the city) produce excellent maps and timetables, and Rover tickets save you considerable sums if you plan to use buses a lot. The County Council organises special bus services during the summer to enable residents and visitors alike to reach local attractions without having to use the car; the Sherwood Forester bus network is now eight years old, a model that could usefully be copied by many local authorities. Though Nottingham station is on several main lines, the train service within the city is virtually non-existent.

Pedals is Nottingham's local cycle campaign group, and together with a sympathetic county council they have achieved a great deal in terms of cycleways within the city. The County Planning and Transportation Department has produced a series of detailed maps of cycle routes in the network, obtainable from the tourist information office. Cycles can be hired from Nottingham Cycle Company at 207 Carlton Road, and the Discount Cycle Centre at 231 North Sherwood Street.

Energy Initiatives: Don't miss the windmill at Greens Mill (see under 'museums').

Community Initiatives: The city has a long tradition of community service, and details of the many initiatives and facilities available can be obtained from the information desks at the Central Library in Angel Row or the Guildhall in Burton Street. Worth a special mention are the Community Arts Centre in Gregory Boulevard, the venue for a wide range of activities, and the Centre for the Unemployed (which they stress is *not* just for the unemployed) at 66-72 Houndsgate, which runs lots of courses and events and has a homely tea and coffee bar. The co-operative movement is particularly strong in the city; the Nottingham Co-operative Development Agency at Dunkirk Road will be happy to give you up-to-date information.

Health: The Holistic Health Centre at 20 Fletcher Gate (Tel: 0602

585740) offers counselling and treatment, and there is also a Women's Health Information Centre at 32a Shakespeare Street (Tel: 0602 414873). The Institute of Complementary Medicine information telephone number is 0602 618139.

Peace: The Rainbow Centre at 180 Mansfield Road acts as an information centre for peace and human rights issues in the city; there is a library, a small shop, and an information display board. *Peace News*, Britain's longest-running peace newspaper, is also based in Nottingham, at 8 Elm Avenue — help is often appreciated with putting the paper together, but ring first (0602 503587).

Local Directories: The joint local authorities in Nottinghamshire produce a monthly news-sheets called *Leisure News*, and the local evening paper a monthly *What's On in Nottingham*. Nottingham's radical monthly, run by a collective, is called simply *The Magazine*, and tends to be heavy on the arts to the exclusion of most other things.

THE REST OF THE REGION

Regional Tourist Office: Exchequergate, Lincoln LN2 1PZ (Tel: 0522 531521).

Ancient Sites: For stone circle lovers, Derbyshire has three of the country's best-known Bronze Age monuments — Arbor Low at Monyash, west of Bakewell; Eyam Moor (pronounced Eem) six miles north of Bakewell; and the Nine Ladies of Stanton Moor, supposedly petrified for dancing on the Sabbath. Sherwood Forest harbours the origins of more legends than anywhere else in England, and tales of Robin Hood were already part of popular culture in the fourteenth century. As well as the Robin Hood visitor centre at Edwinstow and the much-propped-up Major Oak, you can see Robin Hood's Well beside the A1 a mile south of the junction wiith the A639, Little John's reputed grave in Hathersage churchyard, Maid Marian's ditto at Little Dunmow, and a stone in Kirklees Park marking the place where Robin himself is said to be buried.

Trees and Woodland: In the last forty years the rich farmlands of the East Midlands have lost vast tracts of woodland and hundreds of miles of hedgerow, so that large areas of Lincolnshire and Leicestershire now resemble prairies. In the more rolling upland areas like Belvoir and Rockingham Forests, eighteenth century coverts planted by foxhunting landowners dot the landscape, and more of the hedgerows have been preserved. Only on the poorer soils of Charnwood and Sherwood have any expanses of woodland survived, some high-forest oak though largely replanted in recent

The Shires

years, usually with conifers. Swithland Woods between Leicester and Loughborough retain much of their ancient richness, while Treswell Wood near East Retford in north Nottinghamshire (by permit only from the Nottinghamshire Trust for Nature Conservation — see under 'wildlife') is the sole remaining Midland example of ancient woodland which has been coppiced to the present day. The wood retains a great variety of species, including aspen, wych elm, birch and rowan, with a thick and varied shrub layer.

Wildlife: Apart from the high moors of the Peak District, relative wilderness has given way to human influence in most of the region, though disused canals and gravel pits provide a stopover for large numbers of migrating birds. Odd corners of a de-industrialised landscape — railway cuttings, disused brickworks — also provide a home for rich communities of plants and small animals, while motorway embankments likewise provide undisturbed habitats. Reservoirs like Eye Brook and Rutland Water, while inundating large areas of land, support important nature reserves — since it was constructed in the mid-1970s, the reserve at Rutland Water has attracted over 200 different bird species. The county nature conservation trusts for the area are: Derbyshire Naturalists' Trust (Elvaston Country Park, Derby DE7 3EP); Nottinghamshire TNC (2-12 Warser Gate, Nottingham NG1 1PA); Lincolnshire TNC (Manor House, Alford, Lincolnshire LN13 9DL); and Leicestershire TNC (1 West Street, Leicester LE1 6UU).

Protected Areas: Most of the Peak District National Park, the first English national park to be designated (in 1951), lies within the region. The southern part is called The White Peak, because the underlying rock is limestone; here the landscape is for the most part green and undulating. The Dark Peak of the northern half overlies millstone grit, an area of imposing escarpments and wild sepia moors. Surrounded as it is by the cities of Yorkshire and Lancashire, the area is the wild playground for large numbers of people, and the 'honeypots' can be very crowded in summer; the park is also under constant threat from mining and quarrying, and from road developments, though a plan to run a motorway across the middle of the park from Sheffield to Manchester now appears to have been shelved. Information about the park can be obtained from the National Park office at Aldern House, Baslow Road, Bakewell. Further east, a large part of the relatively unspoilt Lincolnshire Wolds were made an Area of Outstanding Natural Beauty in 1973; the Wolds Way (see under 'access') was opened during the same period.

Access to the Countryside: In the more peopled parts of the region

The Shires

access to the countryside is limited to public footpaths, though the footpath network in most places is fairly dense; canal towpaths and disused railways often provide good and varied walking. After the Lake District, access to the Derbyshire hills is as free as anywhere in England, thanks largely to access agreements made between landowners and the national park authority; the authority has also played a large part in converting old railway lines in the park into long distance paths — leaflets about the Sett Valley Trail and the Tissington and High Peak Trails are available from tourist information offices. Other long-distance paths in the region include the 140-mile-long Viking Way through Lincolnshire (set of 6 leaflets and a booklet from Lincolnshire County Council, County Offices, Lincoln LN1 1YL) and the Cal-der-went Walk in north Derbyshire (booklet available locally).

Organic Initiatives: In response to growing demand, a number of farmers in the region, especially in Lincolnshire, are beginning to move towards producing organic produce. On the fruit and vegetable side, Chevelswarde Organic Growers at The Belt, South Kilworth, Lutterworth sell a good range, while at North Scarle in Lincolnshire you will find at Red House Farm one of the country's foremost suppliers of organically and humanely reared meat.

Local Building Traditions: Apart from the Peak District and the limestone escarpment of the south-east, where local stone predominates, the most common building material in the region is brick, though some early timber-framed houses have survived, and you will still see the occasional thatched cottage. Many local museums are housed in listed buildings, and the region's churches reflect its agricultural wealth — the East Midlands contains over a quarter of England's Grade 1 listed churches.

Museums: The Museum of Lincolnshire Life in Lincoln and the Stoke Bruerne Rural Life Museum near Towcester both have large collections depicting local crafts and skills. The Stoke Bruerne Museum is alongside the excellent Waterways Museum (both are beside the Grand Union Canal), and a joint ticket can be obtained for both. Other 'green transport' museums are the National Cycle Museum at Brayford Wharf in Lincoln, and the National Tramway Museum at Crich, near Matlock in Derbyshire. Of the many other specialist collections, two which are particularly fascinating are the Bellfoundry Museum in Loughborough and the Cottage Music Museum at Whaplode St Catherine, near Spalding, the official museum of the Fairground Society. Finally, Church Farm Museum near Skegness is a friendly farm life museum centred around a traditional farmhouse and its outbuildings.

The Shires

Community Initiatives

Community Housing and Architecture: The most interesting community regeneration initiative in the region in recent years has been at Wirksworth in Derbyshire, where a decaying and demoralised quarry town has been transformed in the last eight years. Seed money from the Civic Trust helped to stimulate local interest in the town, its heritage and its potential. The environment has been cleaned up, several hundred new jobs created, and community spirit revived. A walk round Wirksworth and a visit to its Heritage Centre are visible proof of what can be achieved given community will and involvement.

Other Community Activities: Monyash in Derbyshire has since 1981 been the location of an imaginative venture in integrated rural development, a Common Market funded community project to revitalise a stagnant local economy in an ecologically and socially sound way. Management grants have been used to conserve important elements of the landscape, while appropriate small-scale tourist and industrial development have been encouraged.

In another area of green concern, Leicestershire has always been a county willing to try brave experiments in the educational field, pioneering truly comprehensive education and community colleges. One way of finding out about radical education in England today, and especially in the area where it was first put into practice on a large scale, is to read *Libertarian Education*, put together by a local collective (LibEd, The Green, Leire, Leicestershire LE17 5HL).

Communal Groups: In and around Leicester is the group called Some People, a network of friends who want to live more co-operatively. Among other things they organise a car-share, a land trust and an income pool; they welcome interested visitors, though do write first to 12 Bartholemew Street, Leicester LE2 1FA.

Economic Initiatives

Co-operatives: Co-operatives are not thick on the ground in this generally well-off part of England, though Wellingborough is the home of one of the country's earliest and largest co-ownership companies, the Scott Bader Company, brought to wide public attention by Fritz Schumacher in his *Small is Beautiful*. Arts co-operatives are well represented in the area, including several theatre companies.

Craft Workshops: The regional tourist board's *Guide to the Shires of Middle England* contains a full list of craft centres, of which there are over a dozen, not to mention individual craftspeople working and showing their wares. The most interesting and varied centres are at Caudswell's Mill, Matlock; Eastwood Craft Centre near Nottingham (a range of converted workshops near to D.H. Lawrence's birthplace); Longdale Rural Craft Centre at Ravenshead

The Shires

near Mansfield, and Rufford Craft Centre, set in a country park near Newark.

Transport: Long distance rail services in the area are reasonable, though many branch lines were closed in the 1960s. Recent rail lobby successes in the region include the reopening of the Kettering-Corby line to passenger traffic. Nottinghamshire has been particularly forward-looking in providing an integrated public transport system; the guide to its Special Bus Network is a model of clarity.

Despite the heavy traffic on the region's main roads, there are enough back roads to make cycling a worthwhile option. The regional tourist board can supply a list of cycle hirers and tour organisers, while a very good and detailed guide to cycle hire in the Peak District national park is available from local tourist information offices.

Energy Initiatives

Nuclear and Anti-Nuclear: Nuclear waste dumping is the most immediate issue to the inhabitants of the region; the Lincolnshire and Nottinghamshire Against Nuclear Dumping campaign can be contacted at The Wharf, Trent Lane, Collingham, Newark.

Alternative Energy: A century ago, windmills were an essential element of the Lincolnshire landscape. Heckington windmill near Sleaford is a unique surviving example of an eight-sail mill, while you can see traditional restored six-sail mills at Sibsey near Boston (the Sibsey Trader Mill), Burgh le Marsh near Skegness, and Alford near Lincoln. Caudwell's Mill near Matlock (see also 'craft centres') is a working watermill.

Health: See the 'health' section under Nottingham. You will also find natural health centres which offer a reasonable range of therapies at Glossop (Glossop Healing Centre, 3 Spinney Close; Tel: 04574 3563), Chesterfield (Natural Therapy Centre, 21 Derby Road; Tel: 0246 71500), Loughborough (Loughborough Health Clinic, 31 Biggin Street), and Oakham (The Ark, Westfield Avenue; Tel: 0372 55776).

Food: Cheese and cake are the region's best-known specialities. Red Leicester and Stilton are excellent local cheeses; the latter can only legitimately be made in Leicestershire (its original home), Nottinghamshire and Derbyshire, and you can visit the Long Clawson Dairy near Melton Mowbray to see it being made. Gingerbread (named after various towns where the recipe is said to have been compiled) and Bakewell Pudding (a delicious combination of pastry, sponge and jam) are the region's temptations to sugar addicts.

East Anglia

East Anglia is not an easy region for a visitor to get to know. There are few hills to provide vantage points, and its charm, being small scale, often leads those who know it only fleetingly to dismiss it as boring. While relative flatness is the feature that the four eastern counties have in common, once you have experienced the ocean-like expanse of the Fens, the reedy intimacy of the Broads, the

East Anglia

forests of Breckland, and the grand parks of west Suffolk, you will find it hard to concur with that harsh judgement.

Most travellers head straight for Cambridge or Norwich; a few find their way to St Etheldreda's magnificent cathedral at Ely, the wharves at Lynn where 'Revolution' was filmed, the nature reserves of the north Norfolk coast, or the proud 'wool churches' around Lavenham. To appreciate its true nature, however, East Anglia is a country for walking and cycling: you can hire bikes in all the main towns, and long distance footpaths enable you to trace the ancient trackways of the region.

South Essex is really London's northern suburbia, and the mock-Tudor and privet hedges have long since engulfed towns like Chelmsford and Southend. Having traditionally been an ultra-rural backwater, the rest of East Anglia is now suffering from its relative proximity to the capital, with property prices rising faster here than in any other part of the country, and rural communities being swamped by incomers. The army and the Forestry Commission have between them effectively sealed off most of the heathlands of western Norfolk, and intensive agriculture has bequeathed some of the most nitrate-polluted groundwater in England.

Yet there are still many unspoilt corners of East Anglia, and even though you must ignore the housing estates and silos on the way, you can still see Dedham Vale much as it was when Constable painted his great 'six-footers', or Cornard Wood as Thomas Gainsborough painted it. Ely's octagonal lantern tower is the same feat of timber engineering as it was six hundred years ago, Norwich's Elm Hill is still essentially medieval in its appearance, and if chemical dumping in the North Sea can at last be contained, the haunting saltmarshes of East Anglia's unique coastline will survive for future generations of seabirds and children to enjoy.

East Anglia

NORWICH

For a couple of hundred years until around 1700, Norwich was England's second city, and it proably retains more of its medieval buildings and character than anywhere else in the country. If you climb St James Hill in the park at Mousehold Heath, you get a good impression of the narrow streets and little houses clustered around the cathedral and the Norman castle; only in the west around Pottergate and Grapes Hill, where remnants of the flint-built city wall sit uneasily alongside the ugly dual carriageway, have unfeeling developers had their way.

Norwich has always been a pioneering city, and this has continued into the twentieth century with green-tinted initiatives like England's first pedestrian precinct, the earliest regional folk museum (Strangers Hall in Charing Cross), and the first new English university to have ecologically-landscaped grounds. Norwich is a centre of the British peace movement, a city of many cyclists, and a cultural centre with few equals among English provincial cities.

Norwich's tourist information office is particularly helpful, as is the nearby Central Library, which holds an excellent collection of local material. A 'town trail' (with an accompanying booklet) will give you a good taste of the city, which unlike so many places is a real pleasure to walk in.

Tourist Information Office: Guildhall, Gaol Hill (Tel: 0603 666071).

Wholefood Restaurants: There are two obvious choices for eating out healthily in Norwich. If you want a full meal, try Eat Naturally at 11 Wensum Street (good puddings, too); if you want an all-round experience in the place where the lively and intelligent meet for coffee, however, then make for Reeves Yard in St Benedict's Street, where you will find the Café at Premises. Cheap soups and salads are the staples here, and if you are lucky you will also find music, dancing, theatre or craft stalls — right in the café. Other vegetarian eating places include the Mange-Tout at 24 White Lion Street and Tastes (wholefood shop attached) at 46 St Benedict's Street. Lloyds at 66 London Street, while not wholly vegetarian, is a

East Anglia

worker's co-operative serving good food at reasonable prices. If you just want a break, a cup of tea and a chat, visit the Drop-In Centre at All Saints Church, All Saints Green — a very friendly place.

Wholefood Shops: Buying wholefoods in Norwich is not a problem; good ranges and green principles are most to the fore at Rainbow, 16 Dove Street (organics very much in evidence; adjoining café) and at Renaissance, 4 St Benedict's Street (very good prices).

Bookshops: Freewheel Community Bookshop at 54-56 King Street has a full range of green and radical titles, while the Black Horse Bookshop at 8 and 10 Wensum Street is an independent with an excellent range of East Anglian books. The university student union's secondhand bookshop, Mondays-Fridays during termtime at University House, is a good place to find more academic titles.

Museums: The Strangers Hall folk museum and the Bridewell Museum of rural and local crafts are both worth a visit, while the Norwich School of Art Gallery in St George's Street and the gallery at the Assembly House in Theatre Street often show exhibitions of local work.

Shops and Crafts: Norwich has an excellent market, held every day except Sunday in front of the City Hall, and there is a Saturday craft market at St Andrews Hall in St Andrews Street. The Third World Centre at 38 and 40 Exchange Street has equal opportunity Third World goods, and of the many craft and ethnic shops in the city, Paul Wu at St John Maddermarket deserves a visit for his vast range of Chinese crafts. Ward and Wright at 7 Timber Hill make excellent sandals, and the Mustard Shop in Bridewell Alley incorporates a small museum describing this important local product.

City Wildspaces: Norwich has several parks, the largest being Mousehold Heath, a tract of land close to the city centre, much of which is kept as wild as visitor pressure will allow. There are walks along the River Wensum from Carrow Bridge to Hellesdon and along the Yare from Eaton Marshes to the University, where you can visit the Sainsbury Centre with its impressive collection of modern art. The city Amenities Department produces a leaflet for the Yare Walk, and a series about the city's different parks and what you can do there — ask for them at the tourist information office.

Transport: There are good integrated minibus services within the city: details from Eastern Counties bus company at the Thorpe Road bus station. Water buses run on the Wensum in summer from near the railway station to Elm Hill. There are several signposted

East Anglia

cycle routes, especially in the direction of the university, and bikes can be hired from Dodgers at 69 Trinity Street or Magpie's Nest at 112 Magpie Road. *Cycle Rides in Norfolk starting from Norwich* is a useful booklet published by the local branch of the Cyclists Touring Club.

Community Initiatives: The Charing Cross Centre at St John Maddermarket houses a number of community organisations, and should be able to point you in the direction of projects in your particular field of interest. Arts centres at Reeves Yard, St Benedict's Street and St Gregory's in Pottergate often house exhibitions and performances, while Cinema City in St Andrews Street shows good foreign and 'fringe' films.

Health: Though there is a reasonable scatter of complementary practitioners in and around the city, there is no holistic health centre. The Institute for Complementary Medicine information number for this part of the world is 095 389 (Carleton Rode) 505.

Peace: The information centre for the many peace activities going on in the city is The Greenhouse at 48 Bethel Street (Tel: 0603 631007); every Friday noon there are prayers for peace at the All Saints Centre in Westlegate. The Norwich Buddhist Centre runs a programme of events at 41a All Saints Green, and you will find Norwich's Peace Pillar in Chapelfield Gardens (also a beautiful and fascinating handmade clock).

Local Directories: *City Wise* is the monthly radical what's-on magazine, run by a workers' co-operative and well worth supporting.

CAMBRIDGE

One of England's tourist meccas, Cambridge certainly has a great deal of historical picturesqueness to offer. Much of the city centre revolves around the university, so depending on whether you want to see this aspect of the real Cambridge, you can decide whether or not to visit in term time. Though the colleges and their delightful grounds have given the city much of its architectural heritage and its open space, Cambridge is more than just the colleges, and it is well worth walking out along the river, or across Parkers Piece to the delights of Mill Road.

Despite frequent protestations to the contrary, Cambridge is a privileged upper middle class city, its progressive socialist council receiving its mandate largely

East Anglia

from radical professionals rather than from a traditional working class. This means that facilities like museums, libraries and the arts are well developed and supported, yet there has been little concerted effort, for example, to provide a co-ordinated public transport system and keep traffic out of the city centre.

In the supposedly pedestrian precincts of Trinity Street and the Market Square, however, you are most likely to be trampled underfoot by the other visitors or run down by careless cyclists. The best time of year to visit Cambridge is in the autumn, when the backs will be almost tourist-free, and you can see the splendour of Kings College Chapel (try to get to the 5.30 sung evensong) without the company of several hundred other camera-popping tourists.

Of the many tourist guides to Cambridge, the one that tells you the really useful things is *Oliver's Guide*, a £1.95 foldout map annotated with everything from architectural gems to where the latest post goes from.

Tourist Information Office: Wheeler Street (Tel: 0223 322640); usually very busy and rather badly laid out. The reference section of the Central Library in Lion Yard is an excellent — and much quieter — place to pick up leaflets about what's happening in the city.

Wholefood Restaurants: It isn't difficult to get decent food in Cambridge. Nettles in St Edward's Passage provides very good vegetarian food, though the surroundings are a bit cramped. Hobbs Pavilion, overlooking Parker's Piece, is a lovely place to enjoy a pancake and a salad, while if you crave after sugary cakes, Fitzbillies on Trumpington Street is considered by many to have the best in the world — walk it off in nearby Pembroke College gardens afterwards!

Wholefood Shops: Arjuna at 12 Mill Road is the place to get all your wholefood needs — they bake their own bread, and everything is as ecologically and politically sound as it can possibly be — some books too, and notices about upcoming events.

Bookshops: Too many to enumerate, both new and secondhand, but do visit the city's radical and green bookshop, Grapevine in the old Dales Brewery in Gwydir Street — a wide selection, especially of magazines and leaflets.

East Anglia

Museums: Of a dozen museums, the most fascinating and all-inclusive is the Cambridge and County Folk Museum in Castle Street, just the other side of Magdalene Bridge, with displays showing three centuries of Cambridgeshire life and work.

Shops and Crafts: Little shops selling beautiful things abound, but several craftspeople sell their wares in the Cobble Yard Craft Centre, including bookbinders and shoemakers; you'll find Cobble Yard off the new Grafton Centre at the end of Fitzroy Street.

City Wildspaces: Being so small, Cambridge is a very easy city to get out of. A walk along the River Cam to Grantchester (picnic in hand) is a favourite occupation for a summer's day, or take the bus southwards to Wandlebury Ring, which offers good views over the city. At Wicken Fen, England's oldest designated nature reserve, the National Trust has laid out an interesting nature trail, and the information centre has leaflets and an informative display. Both Cambridgeshire Wildlife Trust (5 Fulbourn Manor, Fulbourn, Cambridge CB1 5BN) and Cambridgeshire County Council's Country Centre (Whitehouse Lane, Huntingdon Road, Cambridge CB3 0LX) run frequent outings and events. The local branch of the Rambler's Association has produced a booklet of *Walks in South Cambridgeshire*, £1.95 from information centres.

Transport: Cambus operate bus services within and around Cambridge; the rather tatty information office at Drummer Street bus station has timetables. An Explorer ticket gives you unlimited travel on any one day at £3. Cambridge is very much a city of bicycles, with a well-developed network of cycleways. *Cycle City* is a £1.95 booklet prepared by Cambridge Friends of the Earth (obtainable from tourist information or the central library), giving details of the many cycle shops offering repairs and bicycles for hire; Mikes Bikes at 28 Mill Road is considered one of the best.

Children: If you are travelling with children, look out for *The Family Guide to Cambridge* (£2.40), full of useful information. Even better value for money is the City Council's *Under Fives Handbook*, designed for people who live in Cambridge but useful for visitors too — from the city library information section for 25p.

Community Initiatives: The co-operative movement in Cambridge is well-organised, producing its own newsletter (from Cambridge CDA, 71a Lensfield Road, Cambridge CB2 2EN). Co-ops in Cambridge include Arjuna Wholefoods and The Works theatre group — look out for their audience-participative productions. The residents of Ditton Fields, an eastern suburb of the city, have created a village green and play park project which recently won a Community Enterprise Award — go and see the remarkable elephant sculptures.

Health: Surprisingly, the city has no obvious centre for holistic health, though practitioners are thick on the ground. See *Greenwave* (below) for a comprehensive and up-to-date list.

Local Directories: *Greenwave* is a quarterly local magazine about green issues; each issue contains a comprehensive directory and list of events.

THE REST OF THE REGION

Regional Tourist Office: East Anglia Tourist Board, Toppesfield Hall, Hadleigh, Suffolk IP7 7DN (Tel: 0473 822922).

Ancient Sites: Lacking hills and hard rock, East Anglia does not possess the mighty earthworks and megaliths of western England; its memorials of past times tend to be more domestic and less dramatic. They range from the unique neolithic flint mines at Grimes Graves near Thetford in Norfolk to the fine medieval barn, Prior's Hall Barn, at Widdington in Essex; from the ancient earthen bank of the Devil's Dyke near Newmarket to the old packhorse bridge not far away at Moulton in Suffolk. This is a region of dark legend, too: Wayland Wood, near Watton in Norfolk (now a nature reserve with access by permit only), is the original location of the Babes in the Wood story, while a spectral black dog called Shuck (from the Old English 'scucca', a demon) has been seen for centuries around Bungay. A weathervane near the Butter Cross depicts Bungay's black dog, as does a carving in St Mary's Church.

Trees and Woodland: The largest areas of trees in the region are stands of conifers planted by the Forestry Commission on the sandy soils of the Brecklands around Thetford and near the Suffolk coast at Tunstall and Rendlesham; though there are picnic areas and forest walks, these forests are monotonous and ecologically barren. Much of the region was already substantially deforested five hundred years ago; south Cambridgeshire, for example, still has nearly as much woodland now as it did at the Norman Conquest. Oak and ash with coppiced hazel as the shrub layer was the traditional East Anglian woodland combination, and several large woods are again being actively managed and coppiced to retain their character and richness of wildlife. Some, like Hayley Wood in Cambridgeshire (permit only), Norsey Wood near Basildon in Essex, and Bradfield Woods near Bury St Edmunds, have never been cleared and replanted, so represent fragments of the original wildwood. 280 different flowering plants have been recorded at Hayley Wood, and more than 350 at Bradfield, together with a rich fauna including lizards, snakes, weasel and stoat.

East Anglia

Wildlife: Where wildlife is concerned, the two most important parts of the region are the long low coastline, a paradise for wildfowl, seabirds and waders, and the sandy Brecklands of western Norfolk and Suffolk. The coastal reserves from Snettisham in Norfolk to Leigh on the Thames estuary attract birdwatchers by the thousand; Minsmere in Suffolk, a Royal Society for the Protection of Birds sanctuary, is the best known and most visited — more than 280 species have been recorded here. The Broads around Great Yarmouth and Lowestoft, a feature unique to the region, are described under 'protected areas'. The Breckland supports fascinating plant communities, and several species, like sand spurrey and sandwort, actually thrive on the disturbed soil created by windblown sand and burrowing rabbits. Cavenham Heath near Bury St Edmunds and East Wretham Heath near Thetford are the best places to see the surprisingly rich flora of the Breckland. The county conservation trusts in the region are the Cambridgeshire and Isle of Ely Naturalists' Trust (Cambient, 1 Brookside, Cambridge CB2 1JF); Essex Naturalists' Trust (Fingringhoe, Colchester CO5 7DN); Norfolk Naturalists' Trust (72 Cathedral Close, Norwich NR1 4DF); and Suffolk Trust for Nature Conservation (Park Cottage, Saxmundham IP17 1DQ).

Protected Areas: The Norfolk and Suffolk Broads are the largest area of fresh water wetland in the country, and have recently been given some protection under a Broads Authority based in Norwich; they are soon to be elevated to national park status. The Broads consist of an intricate system of waterways and freshwater lakes created over many centuries by the digging of peat and the subsequent flooding of the peat workings. This flooding, caused by a rise in sea level in the thirteenth century, in turn gave rise to a succession of vegetation, from reed and sedge beds to woodland, which again was exploited for timber and roofing material. In recent years the ecology of the Broads has been increasingly threatened by tourist pressure leading to bank erosion and habitat destruction, a reduction in reed cutting which favours tree growth, and agricultural malpractices including nitrate and phosphate pollution and excessive ploughing. After a long campaign by conservationists in the early 1980s, the Halvergate Marshes near Yarmouth were saved from 'improvement' by sponsoring farmers to use only traditional farming methods. The Broadland Conservation Centre near Wroxham has excellent displays and a wetland nature trail cleverly constructed from wooden planking; the Broads Authority also organises an extensive programme of walks and events. Almost all of the Norfolk and Suffolk coasts, together with Dedham Vale in southern Suffolk, have been designated Areas of

East Anglia

Outstanding Natural Beauty, and much of the coastline has also been made a Heritage Coast.

Access to the Countryside: The network of rights of way in the region is generally good, as is signposting, though access away from public paths is almost non-existent except in country parks and similar public open spaces. The Icknield Way, the Peddars Way, the Norfolk Coast Path and the Weavers Way link together to form a long-distance route more than 200 miles long from end to end of the region (guidebooks available; free leaflet on the Weavers Way from Norfolk County Council, County Hall, Norwich NR1 2DH), while the Essex Way (booklet available from East Anglia Tourist Board) runs from Epping Forest to Dedham.

Organic Initiatives: The rural life museums at Stowmarket in Suffolk and Dereham in Norfolk display traditional agricultural methods; the adjacent farm at Dereham has a unique flock of Norfolk horn sheep. At Debenham in Suffolk is the Cyder House, home of Aspalls, who make organic cider, apple juice and vinegar; Copella, another well-known brand of pressed fruit juices, is based at Boxford near Colchester (as yet, however, these are not organic). Swallow Organics at High March Farm, Darsham, near Saxmundham, grow organic vegetables and a range of herbs, while of the many organic smallholdings in Norfolk, both Church Barn Farm at Arminghall Lane, Norwich, and Mangreen Garden near Swardeston usually have a stand at the farm gate with an 'honesty box' to leave your money in. Norfolk Lavender at Caley Mill, Heacham, in west Norfolk, are the only commercial lavender growers in England: their entire crop is grown organically.

Local Building Traditions: The fine limestone of the far west of the region can be seen in the buildings of Cambridge and the towers of Ely cathedral, but this is generally a region devoid of freestone, depending instead on timber and plaster, flint, and brick, each with a centuries-long tradition. The moulded plasterwork of Essex and southern Suffolk, known as pargeting, can be seen in towns like Saffron Walden and Clare, while Norfolk flint, a versatile and extremely hard-wearing material, is to be found in houses and churches throughout the county — the chequered flintwork of Kings Lynn's Guildhall is a striking example. Much Georgian brickwork is to be found in the fen country north of Cambridge, in towns like Wisbech and Downham Market. At the Museum of East Anglian Rural Life at Stowmarket, several old buildings have been carefully re-erected, including a watermill and a smithy.

Museums: The best museums in the region are those depicting rural life in the past. At Cockley Cley, near Swaffham in Norfolk, an

East Anglia

Iceni village of two thousand years ago has been constructed, based on the best available archaeological evidence, while the rural life museums at Basildon in Essex, Stowmarket in Suffolk and Dereham in Norfolk all have lively and extensive displays of more recent historical periods. Working horses and their gear can be seen at the Norfolk Shire Horse Centre at West Runton and at the Museum of the Working Horse at Toppesfield in Essex.

Community Initiatives

Communal Groups: Of several communal groups in the region, Crow Hall at Downham Market and Old Hall at East Bergholt near Colchester both welcome like-minded visitors by prior written arrangement. Old Hall is a large rural community with an organic farm and craft workshops; Crow Hall is more basic, one of the few remaining original 1960s communities.

Economic Initiatives

Co-operatives: Apart from Cambridge and Norwich, co-operative ventures are not thick on the ground in East Anglia, which reflects the region's relative affluence.

Craft Workshops: There are several places in East Anglia where the practitioners of a range of traditional crafts have come together to produce and sell their wares; the premises are sometimes provided by a trust or a local authority; most are commercial developments. At Alby, south of Cromer in Norfolk, you can see the work of over three hundred craftspeople, while the skills of those in residence include weaving, lacemaking, woodcarving, ceramics and jewellery. Wroxham Barns in the heart of Broadland is arranged along similar lines, with a gallery, produce shop, and a dozen craftspeople working on projects from traditional boats to pottery restoring. At Mistley on the banks of the River Stour the Mistley Quay Workshops include a traditional musical instrument maker specialising in harpsichords and spinets, while The Dedham Centre in Essex's Constable country incorporates a gallery of local crafts and a wholefood restaurant. At the rake factory at Little Welnetham near Bury St Edmunds traditional implements are made from the thinnings of the local Bradfield Woods, now a nature reserve, which have been managed since the thirteenth century to provide a sustainable harvest of usable timber. There are guided tours of the factory by arrangement and a leaflet about the woods is available from the reserve's resident warden. Black Sheep at Aylsham in Norfolk produce a wide range of natural fibre garments from their own flock of Welsh mountain sheep, and at Shropham in Norfolk is Grange Farm Recycled Tools, an old threshing barn filled with thousands of refurbished gardening and

East Anglia

building tools for sale — a treasure-house for craftworkers and self-builders.

Energy Initiatives

Nuclear and Anti-Nuclear: At present there are two nuclear power stations in East Anglia: both Bradwell in Essex and Sizewell 'A' in Suffolk are gas-cooled reactors. Following a lengthy public enquiry in 1983 at which much evidence of the risks of a continued nuclear programme was presented, the government nonetheless allowed work to start on Sizewell 'B', a pressurized water reactor to be built alongside the existing station. As part of their new 'open' image the Atomic Energy Authority opened a new visitor centre and viewing gallery at Sizewell 'B' in August 1988. The local anti-nuclear campaign, 'Stop Sizewell', can be contacted at The Greenhouse, 48 Bethel Street, Norwich NR2 1NR, or at Home Farm, Parham, Woodbridge, Suffolk IP13 9NW. Although plans to dump nuclear waste in East Anglia have now officially been shelved following massive public outcry, these plans and the opposition mounted against Sizewell 'B' have produced a powerful anti-nuclear movement in East Anglia. At the other side of the region, at Molesworth in Cambridgeshire, is a US air base housing cruise nuclear missiles until they go home to be destroyed; the base is also home to a more or less permanent peace camp.

Alternative energy: The wind blowing over the low East Anglian landscape has for centuries been harnessed to grind corn and pump water, and the region has the lion's share of Britain's surviving windmills. Wholemeal flour can be bought at Downfield Windmill in Soham, Cambridgeshire, Bardwell Windmill in Suffolk and Thelnetham Windmill near Diss. Sutton Windmill in Norfolk, with its new 73 foot sails, is the tallest in the country, and you can visit all nine floors; Berney Arms Mill on the Halvergate Marshes (see 'protected areas') contains an exhibition of windmills. The Norfolk Windmills Trust has produced a useful booklet called *Windmills to Visit*, available from tourist information offices. The Central Electricity Generating Board has recently announced that the world's first offshore wind generator will be sited off the Norfolk coast — work is planned to start in 1990. The region also boasts several working watermills. You can see flour being ground at Letheringsett Watermill near Holt in Norfolk, Snettisham Watermill near Kings Lynn, and Pakenham Watermill in Suffolk, while at Woodbridge near Ipswich is one of Britain's last remaining tide mills, carefully restored to full working order.

Transport: Though many rural lines have been closed, parts of the region (like east Norfolk) have a reasonable local train service. Rural bus services vary a lot, and timetables and route plans are

East Anglia

hard to come by and difficult to co-ordinate. Eastern Counties (Norwich Bus Station, Thorpe Road) run services in the north of the region; Eastern National (Chelmsford Bus Station, Duke Street) in the south; Premier and United (Cambridge Bus Station, Drummer Street) in the west. East Anglia Tourist Board produces a good free *Cycling and Activity Holidays* booklet, which includes information about cycle hire throughout the region together with details about useful publications and tips for cyclists.

Health: See under Cambridge and Norwich. The Suffolk Natural Health Centre in Ipswich (15 Fonnereau Road; Tel: 0473 58788) also offers a range of therapies including homeopathy, acupuncture and massage. The Institute for Complementary Medicine public information telephone number for the region is 095 389 505.

Food: North Sea herring, lobster and oysters have been enjoyed since Roman times at least, and the long coastline is still famous for its seafood. Samphire, a local marshplant vegetable sometimes called 'poor man's asparagus', features on many menus in early summer. Frumenty, a fruity porridge made from new wheat soaked in milk and water, is a famous Suffolk dish. At Welle Manor Hall in Norfolk near Upwell in Cambridgeshire (guided tours) you can taste the Original Norfolk Punch, made from a galaxy of herbs, while Culpepers the Herbalists grow most of their own herbs at the gardens in Wixoe, Suffolk (visits by appointment). From June until November you will find 'pick your own fruit' signs up all over the region, and you may be able to arrange yourself a cheap holiday by helping to harvest fruit. Look out for Norfolk Biffin apples, traditionally used for drying for winter use.

Bookshops: See under Cambridge and Norwich. After Londoners, East Anglians read more than the inhabitants of any other English region; you will therefore find bookshops fairly thick on the ground. Clock in Lowestoft (138 High Street) is a recently-opened arts and alternatives bookshop.

Local Directories: See under Cambridge and Norwich. *Bodymind* is a small-format magazine-cum-directory listing alternatives in the Chelmsford area of Essex. *What's On in East Anglia* is a useful free monthly, usually available from tourist information offices.

The West Country

For many travellers, England's West Country is *the* real England, and after London it is the most visited part of England. Its attractions are far too numerous to list in a couple of paragraphs, but they include a long and spectacular coastline, rolling hills and traditional villages, a prehistoric landscape second to none, areas of moorland which come as close to wilderness as you will find anywhere in southern England, and a rich network of people involved in green alternatives.

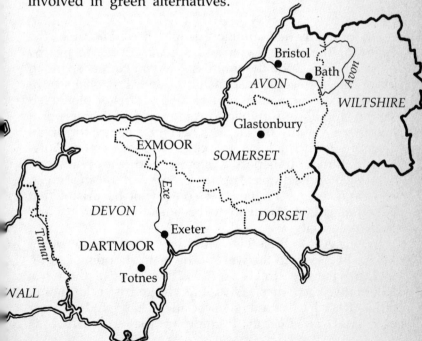

West Country

The gateway towns to the West Country are Bristol, Swindon and Salisbury, and Bristol is in many respects the 'capital' of the region, a good place to start your exploration of the south-west. The West Country is the largest of the English Tourist Board regions, Lands End being more than two hundred miles from Swindon, so do leave time to do it justice.

Bank holidays and the month of August will see traffic jams and crowds at most of the 'attractions', but even at the height of summer you should easily be able to find peace and quiet if you are prepared to be a little adventurous. Tourism is now one of the West Country's main industries, so be prepared for a fairly hard sell if you choose to visit tourist highlights. Again, though, there will always be interesting places and projects to visit if your instinct is to avoid the masses.

BRISTOL

A city of nearly half a million people, Bristol occupies the valley of the River Avon and spreads over the nearby hills, which include the impressive Avon Gorge, spanned by Brunel's graceful suspension bridge. Bristolians have always been innovative and visionary; Bristol pioneered sailing ship design, public education and civic enterprise, and more recently the city has become a centre for urban appropriate technology, the city farms movement, integrated public transport systems, and the renowned Schumacher Lectures. In the process of raising green consciousness in England, it could well be Bristol that edges ahead of Sheffield to become the country's first truly green city.

If your visit to Bristol is a short one, head first for the St Michaels district to the west of the main shopping centre. In these narrow streets you will find most of the city's 'alternative' activities, as well as the tourist information office (the local traders association has produced an excellent free illustrated guide to the area which is

West Country

available from many of the local shops). Given more time you could wander up Park Row towards Whiteladies Road or Clifton, Bristol's most elegant and sought-after suburb with shops and prices to match, or south towards Windmill Hill where you will find Bristol's city farm and urban technology centre.

Tourist Information Office: Colston House, Colston Street (Tel: 0272 293891).

Wholefood Restaurants: Sadly, Bristol's best wholefood restaurant, Wild Oats II, closed in 1988, though it might re-emerge in a new guise. For daytime snacks try the Green Leaf Café at 82 Colston Street, Sunflower at 359 Gloucester Road, or the café at the Rowan Tree in The Triangle.

Wholefood Shops: Rowan Tree also sell wholefoods, as do several other shops in the city, but the highlight in Bristol wholefooding is the Wild Oats shop at 11 Lower Redland Road, which sells an impressive range including macrobiotic and organic ingredients. The Stoneground Bakery at 78-82 Bedminster Parade is the place for excellent bread and bakery goods.

Bookshops: Head straight for Green Leaf Books at 82 Colston Street, which has a good selection of green books and an informative notice board. Full Marks at 37 Stokes Croft, not far from the bus station, is a good socialist bookshop, while Rowan Tree (see under 'restaurants') sells a range of 'new age' titles.

Museums: The City Docks are well worth a visit, as Bristol is a world centre for sailing ship restoration and it is heartening to see a city centre dockland which is still thriving. Still in dockland, the Arnolfini Gallery is a centre for contemporary arts, with a thought-provoking programme of events, while the Industrial Museum will explain the city's manfacturing and trade history. The Exploratory is a fascinating hands-on science display, though entirely mainstream. Blaise Castle House at Henbury is home for a fascinating rural life collection, including a working water mill and country walks with views southwards across the city.

Shops and Crafts: Bristol's main market is at St Nicholas Street (Monday to Saturday); the main shopping centre (though rather boring) in Broadmead. Bristol Craft Centre, which houses 23 different workshops, can be found in Leonard Lane, off Corn Street. Don't miss Biashara at 84 Colston Street, a fascinating Third World shop and education centre.

West Country

City Wildspaces: If you have time, do visit the Windmill Hill City Farm in Philip Street, Bedminster, a shining example for all such projects. The Riverside Garden Centre at the south end of the Avon gorge is much more exciting than its name might suggest, since this is one of Britain's first organic nurseries, together with a pleasant cafe with spectacular views of the gorge. Avon Wildlife Trust is a very active conservation group; their flagship site at Willsbridge Mill on the A431 near Keynsham is well worth a visit, with walks, adventurous exhibits and a full programme of events. Brandon Hill Nature Park, a short walk west of St Michaels, is an impressive city centre open space, while to the north-east the Frome Valley provides a pleasant suburban nature trail (a leaflet is available).

Transport: Bristol's bus service is impressive, with a free 'City Line Overground' map available from bus station and information centre; there are plans for an integrated light rail system, tentatively called Avon Metro. From offices at 35 King Street, Cyclebag and Sustrans co-ordinate cycling initiatives and campaigns — the cycleway along the old railway from Bath to Bristol is one of their early achievements. There is no obvious place for cycle hire in the city — enquire at Cyclebag or the tourist information centre.

Energy Initiatives: If you look carefully you can see the small wind generator on the roof of Low Energy Supply Systems' offices at 84 Colston Street, but for a full array of windmills, solar panels and energy saving demonstrations visit the Bristol Energy Centre's energy-efficient house next to the city farm in Philip Street, Bedminster.

Community Initiatives: The Wool Hall at the north end of St Thomas Street is being developed as a centre for small community-based businesses, while there are plans for a green information bureau and conference centre to be incorporated in the new youth hostel to be built next to the Arnolfini Gallery. The renovation of important small historic houses in the city, including Old Market Street (especially 36-42) and Colston Street (especially 72 and 74), owes much to voluntary community action groups. The Zenzele project in the St Pauls area is an excellent example of the achievement of young people, given help and support, in becoming involved in the provision of their own housing.

Health: Bristol Natural Health Centre at 122 Coldharbour Road, Redland (Tel: 0272 47177) and Bristol Natural Health Clinic at 39 Cotham Hill (Tel: 0272 741199) both offer a range of therapies and can refer you to a local practitioner. Overlooking the river at Clifton is the world-famous Bristol Cancer Help Centre, while CARE, the cancer aftercare society, also has its offices in the city. There is a natural pharmacy called Health Matters under the Natural Health Clinic at 39 Cotham Hill, selling natural remedies and environment-friendly household goods.

Local Directories: Rather suprisingly, there is no local directory of green activities in Bristol, though by the time you read this the Green Pages South West project may have come up with a regional listing. Ask at Green Leaf bookshop.

BATH

Bath, 'The Georgian City', is for the most part beautiful, genteel and monied. It thus attracts hordes of tourists, especially foreign students, so that crossing the Abbey Green on a sunny August afternoon during the Bath Festival can be quite an ordeal. Travel writer Jan Morris wrote of Bath: 'Vivacity does not come naturally to the place. Its setting is picturesque but soporific'. I tend to agree, though there are interesting green initiatives in Bath that are well worth visiting.

Tourist Information Office: Abbey Churchyard (Tel: 0225 62831) — not easy to find.

Wholefood Restaurants: The best is Huckleberry's at 34 Broad Street; also Demuths in North Parade Passage. A slightly upmarket wholefood restaurant, if there were one, would thrive.

Wholefood Shops: Harvest is one of England's oldest wholefood shops, still going strong at 37 Walcot Street. Two good wholefood bakeries are the Broad Street Bakery at 14 Broad Street and Scoff's in Kingsmead Square.

Bookshops: The Bath Alternative Bookshop at 15 Margaret's Buildings, near Royal Crescent, is one of the most attractive and inviting green bookshops in England — don't miss it.

Shops and Crafts: The Food Market is held in The Guildhall (Monday to Saturday). Bath is an excellent shopping centre, with branches of almost every upmarket chain. Don't miss Tumi South American crafts at 8-9 New Bond Street Place, and if you like toys, Tridias at 124 Walcot Street.

City Wildspaces: Bath is surrounded by hills, and is easy to get out of. Brown's Folly Nature Reserve, a couple of miles east of the city, offers a varied landscape and spectacular views (leaflet available).

West Country

Transport: Good network of minibus routes. Cycle hire from John's Bikes, London Road or Avon Valley Cyclery, Dorchester Street (behind the station). The Kennet and Avon Canal is being restored, and you can walk along it for some distance from Pulteney Bridge in the city centre.

Health: As you might imagine, Bath is well served by both mainstream and alternative practitioners. Your first port of call if you need health advice should be the Natural Health Clinic at the far end of James Street West (Tel: 0225 313153); they offer a wide range of treatments and can put you in touch with an appropriate practitioner. Bath has the only natural hot springs in England — the spa water can be sampled if you visit the Pump Rooms.

GLASTONBURY

For many people with a sense of history and mythology, Glastonbury is a magical place. Here are Glastonbury Tor, which some people reckon to be the 'heart chakra' of England; the well where Joseph of Arimathea supposedly buried the chalice used at the Last Supper; the abbey whose geometry supposedly reflects the harmony of the universe; the thorn tree that grew from St Joseph's staff; and the alleged final burial place of King Arthur and Queen Guinevere.

Largely as a result of the magical pull of the place, Glastonbury has developed the most integrated and closely-knit alternative economy and community life of anywhere in England, and the bottom end of the High Street really does have the feel of 'a village within a town'.

Tourist Information Office: 1 Marchant's Buildings, Northload Street (Tel: 0458 32954).

Lower High Street: You can start your visit at the Glastonbury Experience, a collection of little shops occupying a picturesque courtyard on the south side of the street. Here is the Gaia Information Centre; the sweet-smelling apothecary for natural remedies; clothes and knitwear shops; and the back entrance to Ploughshares vegan restaurant, a favourite meeting place. Ploughshares also has a good wholefood shop at number 4. Round the corner in Magdalene Street is Shambhala books and crystals, while opposite Ploughshares is Unique Publications, where you can buy *The Alternative Guide to Glastonbury* and the bimonthly

Glastonbury Communicator.

Next door to Unique is Isis, a new and exciting craft shop; then comes Gothic Image, an excellent bookshop with an enormous and varied stock, including everything in print about Glastonbury. Next door again is The Tribunal, the town's oldest surviving building, and an ancient monument. Almost opposite Gothic Image is the path leading to The Assembly Rooms, housing a café and meeting rooms, while back on the north side and a little further up High Street is yet another wholefood eating place, Rainbow's End at number 17a.

Elsewhere in Glastonbury: The Glastonbury Natural Health Centre is at 31 High Street (though the entrance is round the corner in Archers Way); it offers a wide range of therapies. The Rural Life Museum in Bere Lane is well worth a visit, and visits to the Chalice Well in Chilkwell Street and the Tor are virtually obligatory. The Very Strange Shop in Silver Street is indeed very strange.

The Surrounding Countryside: Glastonbury Conservation Society has produced an excellent little guide called *Glastonbury Footpath Walks*, while slightly further afield are the unique Somerset Levels, the scene of several conservation battles — Somerset County Council has produced a very good leaflet about them, available from the Tourist Information Office. For a town like Glastonbury, it is surprising that nobody hires bicycles; local bus services are adequate but not brilliant.

EXETER

One of Britain's oldest cities, Exeter is for most travellers the gateway to the south-west peninsula. For a city of less than 100,000 people, Exeter offers a great deal for the green traveller, partly because the city serves such a large rural hinterland, partly because the university and tourism between them bring a large and varied itinerant population, partly because of the imagination of its permanent inhabitants.

Like Plymouth, Exeter suffered the destruction of almost all of its city centre in May 1942, which means a proliferation of worthy 1950s red brick and concrete, but the cathedral and its close survived, together with most of Fore Street leading down to the Exe Bridge, and it is this part of Exeter which is most rewarding to walk around.

West Country

Tourist Information Office: Civic Centre, Paris Street (Tel: 0392 265297).

Wholefood Restaurants: Herbies at 15 North Street and Brambles at 31 New Bridge Street are where Exeter greens congregate; the Arts Centre Restaurant in Gandy Street is also good, as is the recently-opened Café behind Global Village at 38 South Street where, weather permitting, you can eat your salad and cake in their delightful rock garden.

Wholefood Shops: The two real wholefood shops in Exeter are City Wholefoods at 14 South Street (who also sell hot and cold snacks) and Seasons at 8 Well Street. Seasons sell a good range of macrobiotic ingredients.

Bookshops: There isn't an alternative bookshop in Exeter, though you shouldn't miss the Greenscene shop at 123 Fore Street and Exeter Peace Shop at 1 Bartholemew Street West. Greenscene sell an excellent range of recycled paper goods alongside magazines, books, crafts and some wholefoods (they will also tell you what you need to know about Exeter's green scene); the Peace Shop (as you would expect from a city that has one of the largest CND groups in Britain) is very well stocked with literature and information.

Museums: The Maritime Museum is well worth a visit, as are the medieval passages which used to supply the city with drinking water. The City Council organises very good walking tours round the old city — for details of all these ask at the Information Centre.

Shops and Crafts: The Salt Cellar at 33 Longbrook Street is an interesting Third World shop with a small café, while Chandni Chowk at the Harlequins Centre in Paul Street also import directly from Third World craft co-operatives. Quayside Crafts offers fifty stalls representing the work of the members of the co-operatively-run Exeter Crafts Guild.

City Wildspaces: Exeter is an easy city to get out of, being surrounded by rolling hills. Six miles west of the city are Dunsford and Meadowhaydown Woods, a nature reserve looked after by the Devon Trust for Nature Conservation (booklet available), while Dawlish Warren is a mecca for ornithologists.

Transport: Public transport by both bus and train is good and easy to find out about — bus timetables from Devon General at the Paris Street Bus Station, local train information from British Rail. There appears to be nobody in the city renting cycles.

Health: Exeter Natural Health Centre at 34a New North Road (Tel: 0392 213159) provides a wide range of therapies and produces an interesting newsletter; Wednesday is women's day, with discount prices and a crèche.

West Country

Local Directories: There is no local directory of things green in Exeter, though the folk at Greenscene will always be happy to help. *The Flying Post*, a monthly radical newsmagazine, shares the distinction with *Leeds Other Paper* of being the longest running community newspaper in Britain — a good source of information. Less radical but also useful is the monthly *Event South West*. If you are travelling with children, look out for *Exeter's Guide for Parents and Children*, a cheap guide to everything the city has to offer for under-15s.

TOTNES

Along with Glastonbury, Totnes is sometimes seen as one of the main centres of 'alternative England', but its alternativeness is very different from that of its mystical counterpart. As well as being a very picturesque and historic little town sloping steeply down to the River Dart, much of the town's more recent fame has come from the proximity of Dartington Hall, for many years at the leading edge of educational and economic experiment. Today the school is no more, and the famous Dartington Glass Company has its factory in Torrington in north Devon. But the Hall is still there with its gardens, hosting important educational events like the Music Summer School, and the hundreds of people attracted to the area in the last forty years by Dartington Hall and similar initiatives ensure that the Dart Valley remains in the forefront of green-tinted activities.

Tourist Information Centre: The Plains (Tel: 0803 863168).

In Totnes: Near the Information Centre in The Plains you will find Totnes Natural Health Centre (Tel: 0803 864587), offering a surprisingly wide range of treatments. Walking up Fore Street towards the archway called East Gate you will pass Arcturus Books at number 55, with a large selection of titles on alternative health and all things mystical. At 10 High Street is Green Shoes, a women's co-operative, and further up on the other side is The Brioche, a favourite wholefood café. Then at 51 The Old Butterwalk is Salago, 'the shop with a difference', selling mostly clothes downstairs but a a wide range of Steiner-influenced books and toys on the first floor.

Moving up into The Narrows (once the narrowest part of the Great West Road), there is the Conker Shoe Shop (more handmade shoes) at 83 High Street, and at 87 is the excellent Willow Restaurant serving only vegetarian wholefood fare. Almost opposite at number 80 is Sacks Wholefoods, which usually has interesting notices about forthcoming events pinned to the front door.

Also worth visiting in Totnes is the Natural History Book Service at 2 Wills Road, one of England's largest selections of books on every aspect of the subject. A favourite with visitors to Totnes is a river trip to Dartmouth, and you can do a circular tour which includes the Dartmouth Steam Railway as well — would that it were *real* public transport and not just a tourist attraction.

Around Totnes: Dartington Arts run a comprehensive programme of performances and workshops at Dartington Hall, where you can also look round the gardens. At the nearby Cider Press Centre you will find branches of Tridias toy shop and Dartington Glass, along with several craft workshops and a welcome Cranks wholefood restaurant — if you visit in August, do be careful not to get trodden underfoot by the mass of tourists.

South Hams District Council and the Slapton Ley Countryside Centre both organise guided walking tours in the area, which is an excellent way of seeing this part of south Devon. Canonteign Country Park (again preferably visited out of season) boasts England's highest waterfall and wonderful views southwards across the Totnes area. Riverford Farm Foods on the Ashburton road usually has a very good selection of organic fruit and vegetables in season, as well as local organic honey and other gastronomic goodies. Venton Mill (see under 'organic initiatives' in the regional directory) is not far to the west of Totnes.

For up-to-date and detailed information about greenish activities in the Totnes area, see if you can find a copy of *The Dart Magazine*.

THE REST OF THE REGION

Regional Tourist Office: West Country Tourist Board, Trinity Court, Southernhay East, Exeter EX1 1QS (Tel: 0392 76351).

Ancient Sites: The south-west corner of England is where all serious seekers of ancient Albion make for, as well they might. Here are some of the finest prehistoric monuments in Europe, associated for centuries with Arthur and Guinevere, Tristan and Iseult, and a galaxy of giants and fairies. Stonehenge, Avebury, Cadbury, Glastonbury Tor, Tintagel Castle and Silbury Hill need little introduction and should not be missed, but especially at the height of summer these places can get very crowded. In west

West Country

Dorset are two stone circles which you can visit free at any time — The Nine Stones at Winterbourne Abbas and the circle at Kingston Russell; the Hurlers, three fine Bronze Age circles, can be found on Craddock Moor near Minions in east Cornwall. Ancient village sites abound on the moors of Cornwall and Devon, as at Chysauster near Penzance and Hound Tor on Dartmoor, both managed by English Heritage. The region's best-known giant is the wonderfully priapic chalk-carved figure at Cerne Abbas in Dorset, while the fairies traditionally inhabit Hackpen Hill in north Wiltshire and Somerset's Blackdown Hills.

Trees and Woodland: Compared with other parts of England, the south-west has retained a good deal of its ancient woodland. Piles Copse and Wistman's Wood have been part of the Dartmoor landscape for centuries, the twisted and gnarled oaks clinging to the moorland slopes, while at Dizzard in Cornwall the oak forest descends down exposed landslip slopes almost to sea level. Many of the region's narrow valleys contain mixed woodland of oak, ash, holly, birch, hazel and alder; nature trails in Cornwall and Devon include the beautiful Lanhydrock Walks near Bodmin, and the fascinating Welcombe and Marsland Valleys in north-west Devon. The woodlands developed on the chalk hills of Somerset are best seen at Ebbor Gorge near Wells, where the lower slopes carry oak and ash over coppiced hazel. Wiltshire's largest ancient forest, Savernake near Marlborough, has been extensively replanted with conifers in recent decades, but you can still find stands of oak and tall beech.

Wildlife: Much of the region is characterised by narrow sheltered valleys, where banked hedges contain a wealth of wildlife: badgers and foxes are not uncommon, and ravens and buzzards fly above old woodlands. Wild flowers have a better chance of survival where agriculture is more traditional, so in the Devon lanes you will find bluebells, primroses, marjoram and orchids, while the chalk grasslands of Wiltshire and Dorset support an array of small brightly-coloured flowers: agrimony, bird's-foot trefoil, ox-eye daisies, centaury, restharrow and harebell. The coastal cliffs of the region support large colonies of seabirds, while saltmarshes and lagoons attract wildfowl and waders. The isolated Isles of Scilly have several sub-species not found elsewhere, including rare butterflies and the tiny Scillies shrew. Such a variety of habitats as the West Country contains cannot be done justice to in a short description, so if wildlife is your interest, write to the relevant county nature conservation trusts for further information: Avon Wildlife Trust (The Old Police Station, 32 Jacob's Wells Road, Bristol BS8 1DR); Cornwall Trust for Nature Conservation (Trendrine, Zennor, St Ives TR26 3BW); Devon Trust for Nature

West Country

Conservation (35 New Bridge Street, Exeter EX4 3AH); Dorset Trust for Nature Conservation (39 Christchurch Road, Bournemouth BH1 3NS); Somerset Trust for Nature Conservation (Fyne Court, Broomfield, Bridgewater TA5 2EQ); Wiltshire Trust for Nature Conservation (19 High Street, Devizes).

Protected Areas: Much of England's south-west has some degree of environmental protection: Dartmoor and Exmoor national parks include the region's largest and highest moorland areas. A third such area, Bodmin Moor, is an Area of Outstanding Natural Beauty, as is most of the coastline from north Devon to Dorset, the Quantock and Mendip Hills in Somerset, Cranborne Chase and the south Wiltshire downs, and the Isles of Scilly. The Cotswold and Chiltern Areas of Outstanding Natural Beauty take in much of north Wiltshire. About three quarters of the region's unique coastline falls under Heritage Coastline legislation.

Dartmoor was one of England's first national parks, designated in 1951, and comes as close as any part of the country to wildness. Wide expanses of high unenclosed plateau are fringed by narrow valleys where the moorland streams cascade through rocky gorges and steep woodlands. Exmoor is a smaller park, with a spectacular northern coastline. The threats to both parks are similar, the main ones being tourist pressure and agricultural 'improvement', though Dartmoor has the added issue of military use: half of the central moorland remains out of bounds to the public for most of the year; only during August is it open for more than a couple of days at a time.

Access to the Countryside: The rights of way network in the region is reasonably comprehensive, though 'private' notices accompany many of the rural retreats of the urban rich. The army has restricted public access to some of the region's upland areas; as well as Dartmoor (see 'protected areas') the Ministry of Defence has the sole use of large areas of Salisbury Plain in Wiltshire. They have the audacity to say that they are thereby 'protecting the wildlife of the area against excessive human pressure'. Popular long-distance footpaths provide a coastal route all the way from Minehead in Somerset to Swanage in Dorset (three guidebooks cover the whole route), and there is the hundred-mile Two Moors Way from Ivybridge on the southern fringe of Dartmoor to Lynton on the north Devon coast. The Cotswold Way and the Ridgeway both have their southern termini in north Wiltshire, while shorter walks include the West Mendip Way and the Wansdyke Path. The regional tourist board has produced an excellent leaflet called *Walking in England's West Country*.

Organic Initiatives: Four miles west of Totnes, at Venton Mill, the

West Country

Permaculture Association is in the process of establishing an experimental smallholding based on the principles of self-sustaining agriculture; for more details contact the association at 8 Hunters Moon, Dartington, Totnes TQ9 6JT. The organic movement is strong in the south-west, and among more than fifty small farms using organic techniques two fruit farms that stand out are the Stoneybridge Organic Nursery at Tywardraeth, Par, and the Moorfoot Organic Garden at Denbury, near Newton Abbot in Devon, where the more exotic crops include melons and peaches. Montague Organic Gardens at Shepton Montague, near Wincanton in Somerset, use the raised bed technique to great advantage, while at Upavon near Pewsey in Wiltshire is the famous Rushall Manor Farm, a pioneer in organic farming.

Local Building Traditions: The West Country is a region of stone construction, and mostly of small buildings which blend with the surrounding rolling landscape; even the 'large' houses like Cotehele in Cornwall and Stourhead in Wiltshire, both surrounded by beautiful landscaped gardens, are not overpowering. It is also a region of cathedrals, all much-loved but very different from each other: Salisbury with its graceful spire; Wells with its finely-carved west front; Exeter with its Norman towers and intricate carvings. The medieval Vicar's Close at Wells is a perfect example of architecture which houses a community of interest with style and individuality, while the Wiltshire villages of Bradford-on-Avon and Castle Combe (both now extremely 'desirable') show the golden Bath stone to best advantage.

Museums: The region has several very good industrial museums, the best of which is Morwellham Quay near Tavistock; it gets very crowded on summer weekends, but this open air museum has a wide range of exhibits, many of them hands-on. At Claverton near Bath you can see the 1813 pumping station built to lift water to the Kennet and Avon Canal, while at Camborne in Cornwall is a collection of tin mining equipment. At Wheal Martin Museum near St Austell are several working waterwheels and a nature trail. The British Fisheries Museum at Brixham in Devon traces the history of this important local industry, and the Shoe Museum at Street in Somerset is worth a visit.

Community Initiatives

Community Housing and Architecture: Though Bradford-on-Avon appears to be a thoroughly thriving town, many of its buildings only exist today because the local Preservation Trust has worked for nearly 25 years to rehabilitate delapidated houses and make them available as shops and houses for local people; look out for their efforts in Silver Street, where Silver Street House has been given a new lease of life, and in Market Street, where ten years ago numbers 5-8 were due for demolition.

Other Community Activities: Hartland in north Devon is the home of several green-tinted projects, notably the Small School, a pioneering experiment in community education. So as not to disrupt the day-to-day life of the school, interested visitors should always write beforehand. Ford House, Hartland, is the home of *Resurgence* magazine, the Schumacher Society and Book Club, and the Human Scale Education Movement. If you are interested in new ways of working, and particularly in combatting prevalent views about unemployment, it is worth contacting the Cornwall and Devon Unemployment Resources Network at Bridge House, Courtenay Street, Newton Abbot. CADURN has pioneered advice centres and initiatives, especially for young people, and similar initiatives can learn a lot from their experience.

Communal Groups: Of several communal groups in the region, two are worth special mention because they run comprehensive workshop programmes. Lower Shaw Farm at Shaw, near Swindon SN5 9PJ, and Monkton Wyld Court at Charmouth, Bridport DT6 6DQ will be happy to send you a list of events, and may be able to put interested travellers up for an odd night, though always contact them first. The Beech Hill community near Tiverton in Devon also has occasional courses: their particular interests include crafts and organic gardening.

Economic Initiatives

Co-operatives: South-west co-ops include a group making natural fibre clothes, Koinonia in Wells; several shoemakers (see under Totnes, for example); five theatre groups; and a taxi-cab company in Plymouth called Tower Cabs.

Craft Workshops: Integrated craft workshop projects in the region include the Devizes Craft Centre, Gough's Craft Village at Cheddar, the Moorlands Craft Centre at Haytor in Devon, and the Coach House Craft Centre at Kennack Sands in south Cornwall. Of particular note are the Wheel Craft Workshops at Chudleigh in south Devon, where old mill buildings have been converted into workshops where you can see articles being made and buy them directly from the manufacturers. At Willow Craft Industry, Meare Green Court, Stoke St Gregory, near Taunton, you can see traditional baskets being made from pollarded willows.

Transport: Though you can easily get from one end of the region to the other by train, local services are in general not good; apart from the independent West Somerset Railway, operating England's longest private line from Taunton to Minehead, only two branch lines serve the long north coast. Away from the main urban centres, bus services are not good, though some counties, particularly Somerset, have made an effort to co-ordinate services and produce comprehensive timetables. In Avon and north Somerset, Badgerline Buses have joined forces with the Countryside Commission to produce a series of leaflets about nature walks that can be reached by bus; a very worthwhile initiative. The many hills make for interesting cycling, though look out for speedy drivers on the narrow lanes. Cycle hire shops are thin on the ground, though Adventure Cycles at Malmhead, Kenton, near Exeter, do hire bikes and also run cycling adventure holidays, complete with wholefood cooking and a sauna.

Energy Initiatives

Nuclear and Anti-Nuclear: Hinkley Point 'A' and 'B' nuclear power stations have been disfiguring the Somerset coast for two decades, and there are now plans for a third reactor at the site. This is meeting with very strong opposition, both local and national — the local pressure group is called SHE, or Stop Hinckley Expansion, and you can contact them on 0278 652408.

Alternative energy: Wind and water have traditionally been used for energy in the region for centuries. Mills you can visit include Wilton Windmill near Marlborough, where stone-ground flour is usually for sale, and Hornsbury Watermill at Chard, which also has a local museum. In recent years two medium-size wind generators have been built in the south-west, one above Ilfracombe and a smaller one at Helston, and there are plans for one of England's first 'wind parks' to be built at Cold Northcott, between Camelford and Launceston in north Cornwall. Cornwall is the first area in England to set up a local energy plan. The Cornwall Energy Plan, which is designed to encourage energy conservation and foster local renewable energy resources, is still in its early days; it can be contacted at The Old School, Daniell Road, Truro TR1 2DA.

Health: As well as the centres listed under the towns and cities at the beginning of this chapter, there are also natural health centres at Newquay (Holistic Medical Centre, 12 Mount Wise; Tel: 06373 2686); Penzance (Penzance Natural Health Centre, 53 Morrab Road; Tel: 0736 60522); Plymouth (Plymouth Natural Health Centre, Empacombe, Mount Edgcumbe, Torpoint; Tel: 0548 827304); Truro (Cornwall Natural Health Centre, 23 Frances Street; Tel: 0872 40321); Kingsbridge (The Health Centre, The Quay; Tel: 0548 3551); Newton Abbot (Alternative Clinic, 8 Huxnor Road, Kingskerswell; Tel: 08047 2741); Tiverton (Clinic of Natural Medicine, 11a Bampton Street; Tel: 0884 255117); and Yeovil (Clinic of Complementary Medicine, 40a Princes Street; Tel: 0935 22488).

West Country

Food: Dairy products, cider, fish and cheese are the region's best-known products; you haven't really been to Devon until you've had a proper cream tea. Salmon and trout are local delicacies, but sea-caught mackerel are good, too. Locally-made Cheddar cheese is good (you can buy a whole cheese and have it posted home — Quickes at Newton St Cyres near Exeter are generally considered the best), and at Perry's Mills near Ilminster in Somerset you can see traditional cider being made — free samples available.

Bookshops: See under the towns and cities at the beginning of this chapter. There is a good radical bookshop in Plymouth called In Other Words, to be found at 72 Mutley Plain; IOW is particularly strong on ecological issues.

Local resources: A project called Green Pages South-West is slowly gestating in Bristol; in time it is intended to be a comprehensive database of all green-tinted activities in the region. GPSW can be contacted at 84 Colston Street, Bristol BS1 5BB. The south-west is the only region in England to have its own guide to the growth and human potential movement: *South West Connection* is a free publication which appears three times a year and is available from wholefood shops and holistic health centres. *Dorset-Wise* is an annual listing of environmental, peace and Third World groups in the county, available from green-tinted shops in the area.

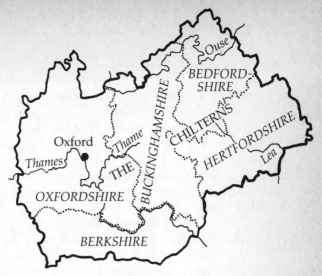

Thames and Chiltern

Known collectively as the Home Counties, this compact region stretches from the suburbs of north and west London to the peaceful north Oxfordshire countryside, largely given over today to the excesses of agribusiness. It includes large areas which have been designated as having outstanding natural beauty — the wooded Chilterns and the soaring Berkshire Downs, together with the most adventurous of England's new towns, from the pre-war

Thames and Chiltern

experiments of Letchworth and Welwyn to the sprawling Milton Keynes, still very much in the process of being constructed. Lines of transport dominate the south-east of the region, roads and railways converging on the gaps in the Chiltern escarpment to carry hordes of London commuters; the builders of motorways, houses (universally called 'homes') and hypermarkets wage a constant battle to have green belt land redesignated so that large sums of money can be made from the region's large, wealthy and mobile population.

Work pulls people into London; the quest for open space draws them back out into the parks and woodlands of Thames-side and Chiltern, into the beechwoods that many say gave Buckinghamshire its name. So thick are the woods that open views are rare, except on the very edge of the escarpment as at Coombe Hill. Hertfordshire and south Buckinghamshire can be usefully visited with a day return from London; the Berkshire Downs and the delightful Vale of White Horse deserve a whole weekend. A day's walking along the Ridgeway, one of England's oldest roads, will show you a fascinating cross-section of the country's pre-history, including West Kennet long barrow, the tall stones of Wayland's Smithy, and the legendary White Horse, said to bring luck to anyone who stands on the eye and wishes. It will also reveal that even the Downs are not free from the threat of tree-destroying grain barons.

Beyond Matthew Arnold's 'dreaming spires' of Oxford, quoted in innumerable guidebooks, is another rural England which, despite modern intrusions, extends in pockets eastwards into north Buckinghamshire and Bedfordshire. This is a farming landscape of low rolling hills and slow tree-lined streams, suffering from agricultural 'improvement' but usually not devastated like parts of East Anglia and Lincolnshire. Then in western Oxfordshire you will find the valleys in the lee of the Cotswold escarpment, where drystone walls replace hedges and grey limestone replaces brick and flint as the traditional building material. North again, in the country around Banbury, iron in the local rocks creates the honey-coloured streets of villages like Wroxton and Great Tew; the same iron also attracts the attention of multinational mining companies.

OXFORD

Oxford and Cambridge, traditional academic rivals, are cities of much the same size, yet Oxford's 'town and gown' distinction is much more obvious than that of Cambridge. Oxford University, the oldest in Europe save for the Sorbonne, dominates the city centre, and from the twelfth century onwards has been endowed with abundant noble patronage, such that the city boasts Europe's first public museum (the Ashmolean), Britain's earliest surviving botanic gardens, and the unparalleled treasures of the Bodleian Library. During term time, more than ten thousand students swell the city's population, filling 'The Broad' and 'The High', the centre's two main streets, with gowns and bicycles.

Yet Oxford is very much an industrial city, too. William Morris set up his bicycle shop in Cowley in 1912, little imagining that his vehicle factory would become one of the country's largest, that the city would give its name to one of England's favourite cars, and that as Lord Nuffield he would be Oxford's most important twentieth-century benefactor.

Considering what an important part tradition plays in its civic life, you might expect Oxford to be a very conservative city. In fact it is in the vanguard of awareness of social and environmental issues. Helped enormously by a 1960s plan to run a bypass through the sacrosanct Christ Church Meadow, a proposal which enraged even the complacent to oppose it, Oxford now has more cycle paths, better public transport provision, and more pedestrian precincts than any other English city of a comparable size. In educational and leisure provision,

Thames and Chiltern

too, Oxford leads the way, and many reasonably well-heeled alternative types find Oxford life most conducive — the city's twenty acupuncturists, for example, must make Oxford's meridians the best-tended in England.

Tourist Information Office: St Aldates (Tel: 0865 726871).

Wholefood Restaurants: Most restaurants in the city now have vegetarian dishes and several serve decent wholefoods. Since Hampsters in Cowley Road closed, there isn't even a half-decent wholefood restaurant in the city, though Brown's at 7 Woodstock Road, neither vegetarian nor 100% wholefood, has good salads and cakes in a delightful period setting. For tea and reasonably healthy snacks, St Aldate's Church Coffee House at 94 St Aldate's is a favourite meeting place; it can get very crowded.

Wholefood Shops: Uhuru at 48 Cowley Road, a women's co-operative, has a very good range, all as politically and ecologically sound as it comes. Neals Yard Wholefood Warehouse in the Golden Cross, off Cornmarket, has a good range, especially of cheeses, and Gibbons at 16 Hertford Street bake excellent organic wholemeal bread.

Bookshops: Oxford probably has more bookshops per head of population than any other English city, most of them owned by the Blackwell family, but if you want to support a very good little bookshop with an excellent range, make your way to 34 Cowley Road, where the Inner Bookshop has one of the country's best selections of green, alternative and spiritual titles.

Museums: Oxford is a city of museums, but worth special mention is the Museum of Oxford at St Aldates, which tells the story of the city from Saxon times onwards; it can get very crowded in summertime.

Shops and Crafts: Oxford's covered market (Monday-Saturday), off the High Street, is well worth visiting, and incorporates many good shops. The Maker's Hand is a collective craft retail centre at 38 Cowley Road, where you can see a wide range of local products. Further up Cowley Road at number 72 is Worldwise, a shop which specialises in Third World crafts and good children's books. Tumi at 2 Little Clarendon Street is a fascinating Latin American craft shop working directly with local producers to encourage fair trading.

City Wildspaces: Oxford is fortunate in having large areas of accessible open space both within and around the city; one of the most rewarding walks is across Port Meadow beside the Thames to Godstow, while Shotover Hill to the east, a country park with

Thames and Chiltern

several informative nature trails (leaflet available from the tourist information office), and Boars Hill to the west both offer spectacular views over the city on a clear day. Oxford City Council is in the process of constructing a new ecology park at Iffley, and the city's countryside department organises a full programme of countryside walks and half-day work parties, on which anybody is welcome: details from tourist information.

Transport: The Travel Shop at 5 Gloucester Street has details of local and long-distance bus services, while the Oxford Bus Company, the city's long-established and faithful original, has an information centre in the High Street at Carfax. During the summer there are regular passenger boat services on the Thames between Folly Bridge, Oxford, and Abingdon, eight miles downstream (though prices are not cheap). Cycling is an obvious way of getting round the city, with plenty of cyclepath provision, and over 1200 cycle parking spaces; cycling has trebled in volume in the last fifteen years. Bikes can be hired from Bee Line, 33 Cowley Road, and Pennyfarthing, 5 George Street.

Energy Initiatives: At The Howe, Watlington, is the alternative energy company Wind and Sun, where you can see (with advance notice) a display of wind generators and solar collectors.

Community Initiatives: Oxford City Council has encouraged citizen participation in renewal schemes, and you can see the results in new residential areas like St Ebbe's and Jericho; the large peripheral 1950s housing estates like Blackbird Leys and Northway have local 'advice shops' to enable people to have a say in policies which affect them. As you might expect, the co-operative movement is strong in the city; many of the projects mentioned in other sections are co-ops, as are a community printing service, Dot Press in Cowley Road, and the Printmakers Co-op at Tyndale Road. There are also two 'managed workspace' trusts, offering small local enterprises space and shared facilities; details of all these projects can be obtained from the Oxfordshire Co-operative Development Agency at 14b Park End Street.

Health: The Helios Centre in the Golden Cross, off Cornmarket, specialises in herbal and homeopathic products, and there is also a treatment room used by several holistic practitioners: ask at the shop for details. They will also be able to tell you about other practitioners in the city (Tel: 0865 245436). The Clarendon Clinic at 12 Winchester Road (Tel: 0865 510636) offers a range of stress-management therapies, and the Isis Centre at Dartington House, Little Clarendon Street (Tel: 0865 56648) offers free emergency counselling. *Oxford Grapevine* (see below) includes a comprehensive directory of local practitioners.

Thames and Chiltern

Local Directories: If you are visiting Oxford and interested in things green, do invest in a copy of *Oxford Grapevine*, an annually updated directory of alternatives in the city and surrounding area. For information about forthcoming events, the free monthly *This Month in Oxford* is invaluable.

THE REST OF THE REGION

Regional Tourist Office: Thames and Chiltern Tourist Board, The Mount House, Church Green, Witney, Oxfordshire OX8 6AZ (Tel: 0993 778800).

Ancient Sites: The chalk hills abound in hilltop forts and burial mounds, while the ancient trackways of Ridgeway and Icknield Street follow the escarpment from south-west to north-east of the region. The Wayland of Wayland's Smithy, the megalithic chambered tomb beside the Ridgeway near Wantage, is the vengeful Norse ironsmith Völundr, a legend at least a thousand years old. In north-west Oxfordshire is the impressive stone circle called the Rollright Stones, high on a ridge with commanding views, and in case you think that London's suburbs have obliterated everything magical in their wake, visit Tewin churchyard near Welwyn. When Lady Anne Grimston died an unbeliever in 1713, her final words were: 'If there is a life hereafter then trees will rend asunder my tomb'; whereupon seven trees, ash and sycamore, proceded to oblige, as you can see. At Weston churchyard near Stevenage are two stones said to mark the grave of a local giant.

Trees and Woodland: Though most of the region lost its original forest cover many centuries ago, you can still see ancient oaks in Windsor Great Park and at Blenheim, and the beechwoods of the Buckinghamshire Chilterns are a joy to walk among, as at Chesham Bois.

Wildlife: Because its underlying rocks are so various — from the heavy clays of the London basin to the ironstone of north Oxfordshire represents millions of years of geological history — habitats and wildlife communities are likewise very different from each other. The Lodge at Sandy in Bedfordshire is the home of the Royal Society for the Protection of Birds; fifty different bird species nest in the surrounding nature reserve. At Thatcham in Berkshire is one of the most important reedbed sites in England, particularly crucial for rare moths. Ivinghoe Beacon, between Tring and Dunstable, is a favourite outing, where from the vantage point of the chalk escarpment you can see for many miles to the north; visitor pressure here can be intense in summer, though the rare

Thames and Chiltern

fragrant orchid can still be seen alongside one of the main paths. For further information, the conservation trusts covering the region are Bedfordshire and Huntingdonshire Wildlife Trust (Priory Country Park, Barkers Lane, Bedford MK41 9SH); and Berkshire, Buckinghamshire and Oxfordshire Naturalists' Trust (BBONT, 3 Church Cowley Road, Rose Hill, Oxford OX4 3JR).

Protected Areas: The North Downs are an Area of Outstanding Natural Beauty, while the London and Oxford green belts have largely succeeded in controlling building at the cities' fringes. What it has caused, however, is intense pressure for development just beyond the green belt, where many recent housing schemes are monotonous in the extreme.

Access to the Countryside: With few exceptions, access is limited to rights of way, though these are generally well-signposted and well used near to urban areas. Further afield, farmers are not so co-operative, and a recent survey of Buckinghamshire footpaths showed that 82% of rural footpaths had been ploughed up or planted. The Ridgeway Path runs from Avebury in Wiltshire to Ivinghoe Beacon (guidebook available), where it links with the Icknield Way Path, heading towards Cambridge. There is an Oxfordshire Way from Bourton-on-the-Water to Henley-on-Thames, and a North Buckinghamshire Way (booklet from the Ramblers Association, 1-5 Wandsworth Road, London SW8 2LJ), while Oxfordshire County Council has established several circular countryside walks in the south of the county. The proposed Thames Path will have most of its length within the region; much of the riverside is already accessible.

Organic Initiatives: The region is the home of two of England's most important organic farming research and education centres, Elm Farm at Hamstead Marshall near Newbury, and Arkley Manor near Barnet in Hertfordshire. Elm Farm is a 230-acre mixed organic holding, while Arkley Manor Farm is the home of the Good Gardener's Association, where the no-dig system of feeding the soil has been developed; both welcome interested visitors with advance notice. Cherry Trees Farm at Ollieberrie Lane, Belsize, Rickmansworth, is a mixed organic farm specialising in free-range organically fed chickens, while Icknield Nurseries at Kingston Stert, Chinnor, Oxfordshire, is an organic fruit farm. Garlands Organic Farm (and farm shop) at Upper Basildon near Reading and Corner Farm at Horton-cum-Studley, north-east of Oxford, grow and deliver organic foods throughout most of the region.

Local Building Traditions: Such a range of building traditions abounds in the region that the best advice is simply to keep your eyes open as you travel round — in Oxfordshire alone you can

Thames and Chiltern

choose between Burford with its grey stone, Ewelme around its fine flint church, and the willowed abbey and curving bridge of Thames-side Dorchester. Cogges Farm Museum, housed in and around the thirteenth century manor house of Cogges, near Witney, takes you on a 'history trail' describing five thousand years of human habitation, while at the other end of the timescale there is a well thought out First Garden City Heritage Museum at 296 Norton Way South in Letchworth. Housed in the architects' office of the visionary duo who campaigned for garden cities, the collection includes much of interest to anybody concerned about the future of our urban environment.

Museums: Apart from the museums already mentioned, the University of Reading's Museum of English Rural Life is well worth a visit. This is one of the largest collections of its kind in England, including a unique display of horse-drawn waggons showing their regional variations.

Community Initiatives

Community Housing and Architecture: Milton Keynes new town, designated in 1967, now accounts for nearly 1% of all of England's new house building. Many ways of building and managing houses have been tried, including several housing co-operatives, and an integrated ecological development called Greentown has been on the drawing board for some time; for details contact the Milton Keynes Development Corporation at 502 Avebury Boulevard, Milton Keynes MK9 3HS.

At the other end of the urban-rural continuum, the village of Ardington, near Wantage, has managed to escape becoming simply a dead dormitory village by providing housing and local work for its residents. Because most of the village belongs to one estate, it was relatively easy to establish a village housing association and support craft workshops and the village shop. There are proposals to convert more redundant farm buildings into houses, workshops and offices.

The Maltings at Chequer Street, St Albans, has been called 'the country's first commercial community architecture scheme'. Developers wanted to create a concrete office-ridden jungle; public involvement has guaranteed that Chequer Street remains a 'proper' street, and that traditional materials like brick and tile blend harmoniously with the rest of the town. The development also includes a library, a health centre, and meeting and games rooms.

Communal Groups: Redfield Community, living in a large house on the edge of the Buckinghamshire village of Winslow, is one of England's largest and most successful communal groups; their activities include gardening, cabinet making and making clothes.

Thames and Chiltern

Redfield welcomes like-minded visitors but they also like advance notice.

Economic Initiatives

Co-operatives: Outside Oxford, co-operatives in the region are thin on the ground, though several small computer and information-based companies have taken this route.

Craft Workshops: In the Oxfordshire Chilterns are two outstanding craft centres, Cross Tree at Filkin and Langston Priory at Kingham. At Cross Tree, housed in a tithe barn and other farm buildings, fine woollen textiles are produced, together with stone-carving, rush and cane work, and furniture restoring. At Langston Priory you can see woodwork, furniture making and printing; a small café provides refreshments. Stable Yard Craft Gallery at Mentmore in Buckinghamshire is a gallery with a difference — all the goods displayed, from basketry and toys to patchwork and stained glass, are hand-made in Britain.

Energy Initiatives

Nuclear and Anti-Nuclear: Though the region has no nuclear power station, it provides the nuclear-capable US air force with two of its largest bases in England. Greenham Common near Newbury in Berkshire, one of two airfields used to site cruise missiles, has also been since 1981 the longest-lived peace camp in the country. The women-only camp always welcomes new faces — you can visit them at Woad Gate, Burys Bank Road, Newbury. Upper Heyford air base in Oxfordshire also has a more or less permanent peace camp at Portway, Camp Road; for details about current activities the contact number is 0869 40321. The region also 'boasts' the Atomic Energy Research Establishment at Harwell, the Atomic Weapons Research Establishment at Aldermaston near Reading, and the Amersham laboratories belonging to the company which manufactures most of the radioisotopes used in Britain.

Alternative Energy: The new town of Milton Keynes is the most important centre of appropriate technology in England. The Network for Alternative Technology and Technology Assessment (NATTA) is based at the Open University, and since 1973 a number of individual houses and housing developments have been built at Milton Keynes incorporating passive solar and other energy-saving features. NATTA (Faculty of Technology, Open University, Walton Hall, Milton Keynes MK7 6AA) has produced a short guide, called *Solar in the City*, to a dozen of the main projects.

Of the many water mills in the region, Kingsbury Mill at St Albans retains the original machinery, and houses an interesting display of traditional farming implements.

Thames and Chiltern

Transport: Public transport in the more built-up parts of the region is generally good, especially on lines into and out of London. In rural areas buses are generally few and not well co-ordinated. Tourist information offices will be able to provide details.

Peace: Milton Keynes is home to one of England's two peace pagodas, built in 1980 by the Nipponzan Myohoji Buddhists. The temple, part of an international network, is at Newlands Farm, Willen Lake.

Health: As well as the therapies available in Oxford, there are also natural health centres at Leighton Buzzard (Radiant Health Clinic, Albion Chambers, 1 High Street; Tel: 0525 372311); Chalfont St Peter (Buckinghamshire Natural Health Centre, Cluny, Winklers Lane); and Witney (Witney Clinic, Church Green; Tel: 0993 73567).

Food: Marmalade and lardy cakes are about all the region can offer in the way of really traditional food; the Frank Cooper Marmalade Museum at 84 High Street, Oxford, is worth a few minutes of anyone's time. Another treat is locally brewed ale at one of the region's still-independent old inns, like The Feathers in Chalfont St Giles or the Crown and Horns at East Ilsley in Berkshire.

Bookshops: Reading's Acorn Bookshop is a lively and well-stocked co-operative, with records, badges and stationery as well as books, and a useful community notice board.

South of England

Comprising the counties of Hampshire, the Isle of Wight, and half of Dorset, the South of England is one of the country's smallest tourist board areas, and its guidebooks and literature often also take in the western half of Dorset and the Salisbury area of Wiltshire, though these are technically in the West Country. The army and the M3 motorway have between them created a semi-urban

sprawl of the north-east corner of the region, while the M27 corridor from Portsmouth to Southampton has done much the same to the south-west. Bournemouth spreads its ugly white bungalows across much of the south-west, while the army at Tyneham and the Central Electricity Generating Board with their nuclear power station at Winfrith have done their best to desecrate the coastal downs of eastern Dorset, Thomas Hardy's beloved 'Egdon Heath'.

Yet away from the main roads and prestige housing developments, the general appearance of the region is of rolling wooded farmland, save when, as the soils become poorer, heathland takes over. In fact Hampshire has more surviving ancient woodland than any other English county: more than 10% of the country's total. There are four varieties of rural landscape in the region: the chalk country of sheep, clouds and celtic earthworks; the green lowlands of watermeadows, thatched cottages and Norman churches; the sandy heathlands of the north-west with their purple heather and bright yellow gorse; and the New Forest, that unique stretch of southern England whose ancient origins give the lie to its name.

The Isle of Wight is almost England in miniature; it was its dollshouse charm that brought Victorian families to its steep little seaside towns, and makes it still the favourite resort for many holiday-makers. Hovercraft and jetfoils have made it accessible to day-trippers, most of whom get no further than the crowded beaches and amusement arcades of Cowes and Ryde, leaving the dramatic clifftop walks and picturesque villages to more adventurous souls.

SOUTHAMPTON

The region has two 'capital cities': the ancient capital of Winchester with six centuries of architecture and a tourist industry to match, and Southampton, more than twice the size, its university and administrative functions making it

South of England

the most important urban centre in the south, and still one of England's major ports.

Considering how much devastation the city suffered during the second world war, a surprising amount of medieval building has survived, especially around Bugle Street. Although some of the rebuilding is good, a great deal is not. Since the reclamation of Millbrook Bay to the west of the Town Wall, the old city centre has looked out on factories, multi-storey hotels and sports centres, while Ocean Village at the other end of the waterfront appears to have been imported direct from California.

Despite the usual strangulation by cars, tourists and lack of public funds, Southampton City Council has worked hard to provide a good quality of environment for the city's inhabitants. Among other things, the city looks after The Common, a large tract of open land gifted in the thirteenth century and still largely wild, and has organised a city-wide network of cycle routes.

Tourist Information Office: Above Bar Shopping Precinct (Tel: 0703 221106).

Wholefood Restaurants: Of several restaurants serving wholefood and vegetarian food, the best is Green Valley at 90 St Mary's Road; the Town House at 61 Oxford Street is passable, and if you find yourself in Ocean Village, the Village Patisserie serves wholeish-food snacks.

Wholefood Shops: Southampton Community Co-op at 92 St Mary's Road sells a good range of wholefoods, including organic fruit and vegetables.

Bookshops: Southampton's radical bookshop is October Books at 4 Onslow Road, where they sell books, postcards, posters, badges and t-shirts. There is also a useful community notice board.

Museums: All four Southampton City museums are worth visiting, and all are free: the Bargate Museum for local history; God's House Tower for archaeology; the Tudor House Museum for cultural history and a peaceful herb garden; and the Maritime Museum, housed in a converted fourteenth century wool warehouse. At Burnham Chase, Bitterne, is The First Gallery, a small art gallery which shows a changing exhibition of local work.

Shops and Crafts: Kingsland Square houses Southampton's covered market, open Thursday to Saturday, the latter being best for fresh produce. Nearby Northam Road has several interesting secondhand and bric-a-brac shops, while at 25 Onslow Road you will find Artisans, selling locally-made crafts together with some Third World products.

City Wildspaces: The 365 acres of the Common makes it the largest of Southampton's many parks, and the Common Studies Centre at Cemetery Road organises a full programme of events; displays and a sales table make a visit to the Centre well worthwhile. Millbrook City Farm at Church Lane, Highfield, welcomes visitors on Sundays and summer Tuesday evenings. Further afield are the Royal Victoria Country Park, where a nature trail takes you through woodland and marsh, and the Upper Hamble Country Park, a mature oak woodland with wonderful banks of primrose and bluebell in springtime.

Transport: Citibus at Portswood Road is the city's efficient bus service; telephone 0703 553011 for schedules. Hampshire Bus serves outlying areas; details from their office at West Marlands Road. The Windsor Terrace bus station and tourist information office also have timetables; the latter will also be able to tell you about ferry services across the Solent.

The city engineer's department has produced a useful booklet called *Cycling in Southampton*, which includes cycle route maps for the whole city together with useful information for cyclists. Bikes can be hired from Peter Hargroves Cycles at 453 Millbrook Road and Cyclemania at 2 Emsworth Road, Shirley.

Community Initiatives: The co-operative movement in Southampton is growing, and includes several of the businesses already mentioned; for details contact Southampton Area Co-operative Development Agency at 56 High Street.

Health: Southampton has two natural health centres, each offering a range of therapies: The Centre for the Study of Alternative Therapies at 51 Bedford Place (Tel: 0703 334752), and Solent Natural Health at 17 Highfield Lane (Tel: 0703 554076).

THE REST OF THE REGION

Regional Tourist Office: Southern Tourist Board, The Old Town Hall, Leigh Road, Eastleigh, Hampshire SO5 4DE (Tel: 0703 616027).

Ancient Sites: Megalith hunters will presumably make a bee-line for the south Wiltshire monuments described in the West Country chapter, but the south has its own treasures. East Dorset has the ruined Norman church of Knowlton set within the circular banks

South of England

of a neolithic 'wood henge'; Christchurch, which legend imbues with a five-headed dragon and the handiwork of Jesus himself; and the grim and luckless castle of Corfe, where King Edward the Martyr was murdered in 978. At Silchester in north Hampshire you can see an almost complete Roman city wall, thought for centuries to be the work of a giant called Onion.

Trees and Woodland: Though Hampshire and Dorset also include heaths, broad downlands and saltmarshes, woodland dominates many of the rolling valleys. The type of woodland depends on the underlying rock. The clay-topped chalk of Selborne Hill, made famous by the naturalist Gilbert White, supports tall oaks and beeches which shade a wide variety of smaller species, including ash, holly, buckthorn, dogwood and spindle. Yew is typical of the chalk downs around Winchester; Old Winchester Hill (leaflet available locally) is a good place to see woodland which, if left to itself, would probably develop into yew forest. Yew can also be seen with beech and oak in the spectacular Wealden Edge Hangars north of Petersfield. The New Forest (see also under 'protected areas') is only about 50% true woodland, but contains a wide variety of species including sycamore, chestnut and Scots pine, with holly being much in evidence. Some of the oaks and beeches are several hundred years old.

Wildlife: Agriculture in the region is very much of the pesticide and fertiliser variety, creating farmland which is inhospitable to most wildlife. This makes the contrast with the semi-wild heaths, chalk grassands and coastal wetlands the more striking. Yateley Common Country Park near Farnborough is a good place to see a variety of heathland habitats (nature trail; leaflet), while the chalk downs of the Isle of Wight, notably Compton Down and Tennyson Down, display an impressive range of dwarf flower species. The harbours of Portsmouth and Langstone (best seen from the footpath along the north shore) are internationally important sites for wintering wildfowl and waders. The local conservation trusts are the Hampshire and Isle of Wight Naturalists' Trust (8 Market Place, Romsey, Hampshire SO5 8NB), and the Dorset Trust for Nature Conservation (39 Christchurch Road, Bournemouth).

Protected Areas: Areas of Outstanding Natural Beauty extend into the north (North Downs), east (South Downs) and west (West Wiltshire Downs and Dorset) of the region, and much of the Isle of Wight has the same status. Though only recently protected by law under Environmentally Sensitive Area legislation, the 141 square miles of the New Forest have survived largely intact, thanks to a combination of poor soils, ownership patterns, and a complex system of common rights. A 1986 landscape survey of the forest summed it up thus: 'There is no area in Britain or indeed in north-west Europe with such an extent of old woodland, with so many old trees, or demonstrating the same lack of intervention over such a long period. Here are mature deciduous woodland, inclosure woodland, open heathland and grass lawns, disposed together to form a complex and attractive mosaic, with the added bonus of numerous grazing animals and a wealth of flora and fauna.' The New Forest Museum and Visitor Centre at Lyndhurst has interesting and informative displays, but you need to walk in the forest to discover its true nature.

Access to the Countryside: Access is generally limited to rights of way, though on the chalk uplands you can usually wander where you will. Long distance paths include the Solent Way from Milford to Emsworth; the Wayfarer's Path from the Solent coast to Inkpen Beacon via Watership Down (of rabbit fame); and the Test Way from Totton near Southampton to Inkpen. The three paths form a circular walk of nearly 170 miles; leaflets are obtainable from Hampshire Recreation, North Hill Close, Andover Road, Winchester SO22 6AQ. Swanage is the eastern end of the Dorset Coast Path, one of the country's most spectacular long walks (guidebook available). Seven Isle of Wight trails include a sixty-mile coastal path (booklets and a rights of way map available from Isle of Wight County Council, County Hall, Newport, Isle of Wight PO31 1UD).

Organic Initiatives: At the Butser Ancient Farm Project (Gravel Hill, Horndean — part of the Queen Elizabeth Country Park) you can see a reconstructed iron age farm which uses organic techniques and ancient crop varieties; after twelve years yields are consistently as high as conventional modern agriculture. The Fordingbridge area of west Hampshire is rapidly becoming a centre for organic growing. Hockeys, at Newtown Farm, South Gorley, is one of the country's leading producers of organic and humanely-reared meat. Next door at Furzehill Farm, vegetables and fruit are grown, while Sandy Balls Organic Gardens at Godshill is an organic herb and vegetable garden.

Local Building Traditions: The grey stone of the region is the almost universal traditional material, though brick was an early introduction, especially for large houses like Breamore, near Fordingbridge — here you can also see displays of turn-of-the-century rural life in an imaginative countryside museum. A common feature of the region's towns and villages is a main street wide enough to turn a coach and horses — Odiham and Alresford are good examples. Out of the tourist season, the Solent-side village of Buckler's Hard is worth seeing; several buildings have been restored to recreate an atmosphere of eighteenth-century life and industry.

South of England

Museums: The Big Four Railway Museum (the 'Big Four' being the Great Western, the Southern, the London and North Eastern, and the London Midland and Scottish) is one of Bournemouth's most worthwhile attractions, while at the other end of the transport scale is the fascinating Tricycle Museum at Christchurch, where the exhibits include the model that Queen Victoria rode around Osborne House well into her old age. The Romany Folklore Museum at Selborne near Alton, collected by a true Romany, is an authentic record of the travelling life. Every good socialist knows that trade unionism was born at Tolpuddle in Dorset, where in 1834 six agricultural labourers were transported to Australia for taking part in an 'illegal oath'. After public outcry they were brought home and allowed to create a union, more than can be said for some of today's workers; the history of the Tolpuddle Martyrs and the early days of trades-unionism is told at the Martyr's Museum in Tolpuddle.

Community Initiatives

Community Activities: At Netley Marsh near Lyndhurst is the main workshop of Tools for Self-Reliance. TFSR organises a national network of people who collect and renovate unwanted hand tools, then send them to Third World villagers and craftspeople; it also organises events at Netley Marsh. Visitors are usually welcome, especially if you want to stay and help.

Communal Groups: At Theldon Grange near Alton in Hampshire, fifteen adults and nineteen children live as a village community, farming 42 acres and coming together for a communal meal once a week. Like-minded people are welcome to visit with advance notice.

Economic Initiatives

Co-operatives: Outside Southampton, there are very few co-ops in the region.

Craft Workshops: There are several integrated craft centres in the region. At Arreton Country Crafts Village near Newport on the Isle of Wight, more than a dozen craftspeople display a wide range of work, while at Viables Craft Centre near Basingstoke the thirteen or so resident workers produce patchwork, engraving, sculptured stones, silk flowers and much more. East Dorset has two such centres: Walford Mill near Wimborne Minster, which displays the wares of members of the Dorset Craft Guild, and the Holt Craft Centre, a co-operative enterprise which also runs a friendly restaurant. Home Farm Craft Workshops at Lockerley, near Romsey, cover a range of crafts including wool-spinning; here Little London Spinners invite you to join one of their short spinning courses.

South of England

Energy Initiatives

Nuclear and Anti-Nuclear: Winfrith in Dorset is one of England's oldest nuclear power stations and the country's only steam-generating heavy water reactor, shortly due for the as-yet-untried process of decommissioning.

Alternative Energy: Eling Tide Mill near Southampton, restored in 1980, is one of the only tide mills in England still in daily use. You can see wholemeal flour being milled and buy it on the premises. Of the region's handful of working watermills, both Sturminster Newton Mill in east Dorset and Botley Mill near Southampton now use a turbine in place of a wheel. Burlesdon Windmill, south-east of Southampton, is currently being restored to working order.

Transport: British Rail's Network South-East reaches as far as Southampton, while 'Wessex Electrics' serve Bournemouth and east Dorset via the New Forest. Bus services are reasonable, operated by several companies, the largest being Hampshire Bus (West Marlands Road, Southampton). The Southern Tourist Board produces a useful bicycle fact sheet, which contains details of cycle hirers throughout the region.

Health: As well as the services available in Southampton, there is a Natural Health Centre in Portsmouth (109 Palmerston Road, Southsea; Tel: 0705 830558), and a large number of practitioners in the Bournemouth/Poole area — the Institute for Complementary Medicine information numbers for Bournemouth are 0202 429647 and 0202 424415.

Food: The two truly local foods are an excellent blue cheese called Blue Vinney, made in Gillingham near Shaftesbury, and the crispy rolls called Dorset Knobs, still made at Morecombelake near Bridport, where you can visit the factory and its adjoining café and art gallery. Watercress is a seasonal delicacy, grown in local watercress beds and eaten fresh from March to September.

The South East

In 1357, King Edward III needed twenty-two guides for the week-long journey through the Weald — the great Forest — from London to Rye on the Sussex coast. Today the fifty-mile trip can be done in an hour and a half. The impenetrable woodland which once covered this great eroded chalk and clay dome went to stoke the iron furnaces of the first industrial revolution and to build the wooden ships which won England the beginnings of its empire. The region's heavy industry has now all but vanished, leaving the South East to intensive agriculture, tourism, and the motorways and housing developments of encroaching commuterland.

South East

The rich soils of Kent have earned it the title of 'The Garden of England', and though badly damaged by the great storm of October 1987, the orchards and hopfields of this corner of England are still important sources of traditional food and drink. The richest soils, however, are to be found under the shadow of the Dungeness nuclear power stations, where massive ancient churches like that at Ivychurch show that the human population was once much greater than it is today.

Long-distance paths along the North and South Downs and across the Weald will still reveal the essential character of the South-East, even if the M25 has encroached on much of the former, and electronically-patrolled entrance drives remind you of what privilege can buy in the England of the 1980s. Away from the London-accessible suburban villages, however — in Ham Street Woods near Ashford, for example, or the extensive chalk downland nature reserve at Wye — you can still imagine what the region might have been like when Edward III made his royal progression.

BRIGHTON

Brighton was a lowly fishing village until Dr Russell (who advocated sea-bathing for every ill) and the Prince Regent (who was responsible for the fairy-palace Royal Pavilion) found it in the eighteenth century. It rapidly became the seaside resort par excellence, with thousands of Londoners taking the train for a summer's day beside the sea. The fine regency houses of the rich and the cobble-built artisan terraces reached up into the flanking denes, and during the nineteenth century Brighton became the urban centre for the whole of Sussex and beyond.

Brighton is still the regional hub for much of the South East, an inspiring mixture of holiday town and cultural centre wedged between the South Downs and the English Channel. Wandering among the shops in the narrow Lanes (but out of season, or you may not come out in one

South East

piece) is a unique experience in contemporary England. Yet for those that take the time to leave the disappointingly stony beach and the souvenir shops, Brighton has far more to offer than many a seaside town, while a stiff walk up on to the Downs will improve your constitution and provide excellent views of the city to the south and Sussex Vale to the north.

Tourist Information Office: Marlborough House, 54 Old Steine (Tel: 0273 23755); also at Sea Front, King's Road.

Wholefood Restaurants: The best of the healthy eating places is Food for Friends in Prince Albert Street — a self-service vegetarian establishment with good food and a big notice board for details of green-tinted activities. Nature's Way at 35 Duke Street and Clouds at 56 Ship Street are also worth trying.

Wholefood Shops: Infinity at 25 North Road were pioneers in English wholefooding, with a comprehensive range from organic grains to their own brand pure fruit juices. Do visit Infinity just for the experience, even if you don't actually need anything.

Bookshops: 'The finest bookshop for its size in the country', said one connoisseur of the Public House Bookshop at 21 Little Preston Street. A good range, and excellent service from a knowledgeable proprietor.

Museums: Brighton's museums are in general not very inspiring. The Sussex Folk Life Room at the Brighton Museum in Church Street is worth a visit, and out of season the conserved downland village of Stanmer, near the University, is a lovely place to walk to. Here is an unspoilt village complete with duckpond, together with a small museum of local rural life.

Shops and Crafts: Upmarket gift shops abound in Brighton. Worth a special mention are The Unicorn Place at 39 Duke Street, an incense-scented new age treasure house, and Java handmade and ethnic clothes at Kensington Arcade. The One World Centre in Western Road (behind Oxfam) and the Brighton Peace Centre at 28 Trafalgar Square both have a range of Third World crafts; the latter also functions as a library and information centre.

City Wildspaces: The city has several municipal parks, notably Preston Park to the north of the railway station, but for real open space take a bus towards the Devil's Dyke or Ditchling Beacon, then walk. Stanmer Park nature trail is even closer to the city (leaflet available).

Transport: Bus services, operated by the Brighton and Hove Bus Company, are good and frequent; the 1 Stop Travel Shop at 16 Old Steine can provide excellent timetables and route maps. The Bus Company is also responsible for a campaign to ease traffic congestion in the city; called Freeway, it proposes street improvements and bus-only lanes. Bricycles — the Brighton Cycling Campaign (27b Clifton Road) — works to promote cycling in the city, and the tourist information office can provide a list of cycle hirers. Harman Hire at 1 Surrey Street are generally considered the best and cheapest.

Energy Initiatives: Not much to see in this field, though windmill enthusiasts won't want to miss the seven-storey West Blatchington mill in Hove, a couple of miles from Brighton city centre. Built around 1820, this wooden smock mill surmounts a typical Sussex flint barn.

Community Initiatives: Co-operatives in Brighton include most of the wholefood outlets and a large print-making studio. Look out for the publications of Queen Spark Books, a lively community publishing house providing an outlet for local literary talent, and if you want to see another face of Brighton, visit the big housing estate at Moolsecoomb, where in the last five years community initiative has established more than fifty different organisations from a credit union to a neighbourhood trust. Don't expect to see too much on the ground as yet, but rest content that the underprivileged of England are not just passive recipients of welfare handouts.

Health: Brighton has one of the best organised and most comprehensive Natural Health Centres in England: the Brighton Natural Health Centre at 27 Regent Street (Tel: 0273 600010). It offers everything from martial arts to juggling; call in for a free programme.

Local Directories: For detailed what's-on information and some attempt at a city-wide directory, pick up a copy of the monthly *The Punter*; for more in-depth analysis of the radical scene in Brighton, *Brighton Voice* is at seventeen years old one of the country's longest running alternative newspapers — it also incorporates an information page.

THE REST OF THE REGION

Regional Tourist Office: South East England Tourist Board, 1 Warwick Park, Tunbridge Wells, Kent TN2 5TA (Tel: 0892 40766).

Ancient Sites: Between the modern estates, hypermarkets and country clubs of the region, you can if you look carefully still find evidence of the land as it was when London was unheard of and the earth was sacred to its human inhabitants. Two miles north of

South East

Maidstone are Kit Coty's House and Little Kit Coty's House, the ruins of prehistoric burial chambers, until the seventeenth century both covered by earth mounds — here King Catigern or Vortigern of the Britons is said to be buried, slain by the Saxons in the fifth century. The Long Man of Wilmington, carved into the chalk of the South Downs near Eastbourne, is also known as 'The Lone and Lanky Man'; sceptics say he is relatively modern (he was recarved in 1874), local tradition that he is a giant slain by a rival who lived on nearby Firle Beacon. The beautiful Silent Pool, a mile or so east of Guildford, is said to be bottomless, an entrance to the underworld; it also boasts the ghost of a maiden called Emma who drowned escaping the unwanted approaches of bad King John.

Land and Agricultural Initiatives: Several demonstration farms in the region are open to visitors. Badsell Park Farm at Matfield near Tonbridge is primarily a fruit farm, though they also function as a centre for rare domestic breeds and have a butterfly breeding programme; a two-mile nature trail leads through woods and meadows. Near Guildford is Loseley Park Farm, home of one of England's best makes of additive-free ice cream; they also keep a number of rare breeds.

Trees and Woodland: Remnants of the great Wealden forest can still be visited, as at Ashdown, the largest single tract of undeveloped land in the region. Fore Wood, near Battle, has been coppiced and harvested for timber and nuts for many centuries; most of the ancient Kentish woodland reserves are visitable only by permit, though you can walk through the yew woods at Westfield between Maidstone and Chatham, and the beech and hazel woods of Yockletts Bank near Canterbury.

Wildlife: The complex geology of the region provides a wide variety of wildlife habitats, though there are few large surviving remnants of relative wilderness. The marshlands in the north and around Romney provide important bird wintering and breeding areas, while ancient hay meadows and unimproved downland give the region a uniquely rich flora — at least five species of orchid, for example, are more abundant here than anywhere else in the country. Human development is a constant threat to the region's wildlife: small reserves like Orlestone Forest in East Kent, which is home to several rare butterflies and moths, must remain closed to the public to prevent further damage. The local nature conservation trusts, who will be happy to provide further information, are Kent NCT (1a Bower Mount Road, Maidstone ME16 8AX); Surrey NCT (Hatchlands, East Clandon, Guildford GU4 7RP); and Sussex NCT (Woods Mill, Henfield, West Sussex BN5 9SD).

South East

Protected Areas: Nearly half the region has been designated Areas of Outstanding Natural Beauty — the Kent Downs, the Surrey Hills, the Sussex Downs, the High Weald, and Chichester Harbour. Beachy Head near Eastbourne, and the chalk cliffs of Dover and Folkstone, are heritage coasts — a fact which has put at least some restriction on the amount of visual impact to be caused during the construction of the Channel Tunnel.

Access to the Countryside: The region has a dense network of footpaths and bridleways, though away from official rights of way the privacy afforded by landownership is usually guarded very jealously. Several long-distance paths cross the region, from the long-established North and South Downs Ways, to the Saxon Shore Way around the Kent coast (guidebook from Kent Rights of Way Council, Lion Yard, Lewson Street, Teynham, Sittingbourne ME9 9JS); the Greensand Way through Surrey (guidebook from Surrey Amenity Council, 2 Jenner Road, Guildford GU1 3PN); and the Forest Way through the Sussex Weald (leaflet from East Sussex County Council, 42 St Anne's Crescent, Lewes).

Organic Initiatives: The rich soil of Kent and Sussex is ideal for organic growing, and several organic gardens can be visited — it's always best to get in touch first though. Two excellent places for organic fruit and vegetables are Marsh Farm Organics at Gore Street, Monkton, near Ramsgate, and Clayton Farm, Newick Lane, Mayfield in East Sussex. The 'pocket garden' at the Maidstone Museum of Kent Rural Life is run entirely organically, and you can also visit England's first entirely organic vineyard at Sedlescombe near Robertsbridge in East Sussex — there is a 'visitor trail' and you can buy wine and other organically-grown produce.

Local Building Traditions: Almost every village in the region still has a handful of timbered and thatched cottages, now very desirable residences indeed. Since no one building material predominates, you will find a wide range of traditional building techniques, from the timber cladding of the Kent coast towns to the stone slates of the high Weald. An excellent place to see this range, apart from walking round the old towns of the region, is at the Weald and Downland Open Air Museum at Singleton, near Chichester, where many buldings from the fifteenth century onwards have been lovingly restored.

Museums: Details of the 150 or so museums in the region are given in the useful *Hundreds of Places to Visit in the South-East*, £1 from the regional tourist board. Of particular interest to the green-tinted traveller will be the open air museums at Sandling, Maidstone (Museum of Kent Rural Life) and Singleton near Chichester (Weald and Downland Open Air Museum — see under 'building traditions'). The Dolphin Yard Sailing Barge Museum at Sittingbourne and the Fishermen's Museum in Hastings recall the seafaring history of the region, while for light relief the Penny Slot Museum on Brighton seafront is a great deal of fun.

Craft Workshops: The regional tourist board produces a good free brochure called *South East England at Work*, which includes up-to-date information about craft workshops you can visit. Craft centres displaying several different crafts can be found at Hernhill, Faversham (spinning, forgework and bellows-making among others); Mill Yard at West Malling (toymaking, picture restoring and knitwear); and Manor Farm at Seale near Farnham (glassblowing, woodturning and jewellery). Traditional wooden products can be seen in the making at Henfield Woodcrafts, West End Lane, Henfield, while at Three Cups Wheelwrights Workshop, Heathfield, you can see traditional wooden wheels being made. At the Truggery at Herstmonceux you can watch traditional chestnut and willow Sussex trug baskets being made.

Community and Co-operative Initiatives: As you might expect in such a true blue corner of England (pockets of the Sussex coast excepted), community-based co-operative projects are thin on the ground in the South-East. In Hastings, however, there are a couple of projects worth visiting. At the Robert Tressell Workshops in Cornwallis Gardens, a disused railway building has been converted into nine small units, mostly for co-operative and community enterprises, while a community project was responsible for the restoration of several traditional fishing net shops on The Stade. One area of green interest that is on the increase is self-built houses — one such venture can be seen at the Sedlescombe organic vineyard (see under 'organic initiatives'), where a timber-framed house was built by trainee novice builders during a workshop designed to teach people the skills needed to build their own shelter.

Transport: British Rail's Network South-East offers a reasonable service, especially in London commuterland, while bus services in the region are good if sometimes badly co-ordinated. Southdown is the main Sussex company (timetables from bus stations at Marine Parade, Worthing; Cavendish Place, Eastbourne; and Southgate, Chichester); East Kent for most of that county (details from Canterbury bus station, Upper Bridge Street).

The South East Tourist Board produces an excellent factsheet about the region for cyclists, covering cycle hire and suggested itineraries.

South East

Energy Initiatives

Nuclear and Anti-Nuclear: Of the two nuclear power stations at Dungeness, visitors are welcome at Dungeness 'A', where by prior arrangement you can look round and be given a friendly cup of tea — the human side of this deadly industry.

Alternative Energy: After East Anglia, the region has the most working windmills in England, including England's oldest, at Outwood near Redhill in Surrey, built in 1665. Among the other windmills that can be visited are the massive Union Mill at Cranbrook (an early example of co-operation between local businesses), and the Shipley Mill near Horsham, the only working smock mill in West Sussex. Richborough, near Sandwich in East Kent, already the site of a small wind generator, has been chosen as for the location of an experimental large wind turbine.

Of several working watermills, the Haxted Mill near Edenbridge is particularly impressive, with its two wheels, while Swanton Mill at Lower Mersham near Ashford also houses a milling museum and is surrounded by extensive gardens.

Health: Alternative and complementary practitioners are thick on the ground in this corner of England. As well as the Brighton Natural Health Centre, there are also natural health centres offering a wide range of therapies and advice at Horsham (Horsham Natural Health Care Centre, 76 Park Street; Tel: 0403 57328), Tunbridge Wells (Wealden Natural Health Clinic, 1 Clanricarde Gardens; Tel: 0892 45443), and Gillingham (Gillingham Natural Health Clinic, 50 Watling Street; Tel: 0643 578844).

Food: For every really traditional regional recipe there are a dozen 'revived' ones, though sponge puddings (Canterbury Pudding, Chichester Pudding, Vectis Pudding . . .) will appeal to sweet-tooths, and seafood dishes like Arundel Mullets have been authenticated at least as far back as the seventeenth century.

Bookshops: There are many small bookshops in this corner of England — Canterbury is a particularly bookish place — though outside Brighton (see the 'bookshop' section under Brighton) there is nothing particularly green-tinted.

London

So many trite statements have been made in tourist guides to London that I hardly dare add to them, but I do like David Benedictus's observation in *The Absolutely Essential Guide to London* that the unkindest cut of all is that after you have been ripped off by ice-cream vendors, souvenir shops *et al*, most guide books insist that, however you might actually be feeling, you *will* have a wonderful time in England's biggest city.

Density of population and density of traffic are London's two most obvious features. Though more than twelve per cent of the area of Greater London is open

space, there is nowhere where you can escape the incessant roar of traffic, and almost nowhere where you can be alone out of doors. There are relatively quiet corners, but for the most part the streets of London are long, hard and noisy.

When you want company, excitement, and the stimulation that goes with fast-lane city living, however, London is hard to beat. There are specialist shops selling everything you could ever want, often at bargain prices. You will find street theatre, galleries and concerts; markets, pubs, and restaurants serving food after the fashion of every corner of the globe. You will also find hordes of fellow travellers, all doing their best to have the wonderful time prescribed by their guidebooks.

In an urban-centred culture like that of England, it is hardly surprising that the headquarters of a large number of organisations and businesses are to be found in London, including most of the larger green-tinted ones. Even the Council for the Protection of Rural England occupies a large office block near Victoria Station. For this reason alone, never mind the sights you might wish to see, the aware traveller will find it hard not to include London in a visit to England.

Cars and people notwithstanding, there are many things in London which are well worth a visit. The main 'attractions' are covered in every tourist guide, and there are a number of specialist guides too, some of which are mentioned below.

If you plan to visit London, you will probably already have some idea of what you want to see. If you have never been before, however, a good place to start is Covent Garden and the Neal Street pedestrian precinct. Even at the height of a hot summer's afternoon Neal's Yard is a haven of greenery and sanity, with co-operative businesses providing wholefood snacks and freshly-squeezed fruit juices. Covent Garden itself, though a little self-consciously chic, usually provides the venue for a range of open-air entertainment, while the shops, market and restaurants in the vicinity are at least a shade greener than most in the city centre.

There is little of note between Hyde Park and the Barbican that hasn't already been milked of its full tourist potential, but you don't have to travel far to find parts of the city occupied by fairly genuine Londoners. Hackney (wander along Hackney Road or up Kingsland High Street to get a feel of it) is an area where generations of immigrants, from Huguenots and Jews to Indians and Bangladeshis have made their new homes; Hackney has recently seen a proliferation of community housing and economic initiatives — Bradbury Street, for example, now houses eighteen worker co-operatives employing more than a hundred people.

For what is left of the truly Cockney East End walk round Aldgate and Whitechapel, pausing awhile at the Petticoat Lane street market in Middlesex Street, the best known of London's many markets. Further east, in Limehouse (travelling on the new Docklands Light Railway), you can see England's inner city crisis in microcosm, an area with a strong community spirit and enormous potential, yet paralysed by paternalistic bureaucracy and warped commercialism — read chapter 3 of Nick Wates and Charles Knevitt's paperback *Community Architecture* (Penguin, 1987, £4.95) before you go.

Another green-tinted corner of London is the area north of Camden underground station and westwards into Primrose Hill. A walk along Chalk Farm Road will take you past Compendium alternative bookshop, Camden Lock Market, Tumi South American crafts and the renowned Marine Ices, as well as offering pleasant walks along the Regents Canal and across Primrose Hill towards Regents Park.

The best time to see the heart of London, traditionally known as The City, is on a Sunday morning when the stockbrokers are in bed or playing golf. Though it has been much desecrated by heartless developers, there are still some architectural gems such as Lincoln's Inn and the

London

fifteenth century St Ethelburga's Church near the Stock Exchange.

Given more time and a yearning for open space, try Hampstead Heath (where if you stick your fingers in your ears you can imagine yourself in the countryside); Greenwich with its observatory, Maritime Museum, and the sailing ship The Cutty Sark; or a walk along the Thames at Strand-on-the-Green, ending up in a tasteful riverside pub like the Bell and Crown.

London is large, and most Londoners tend to stick to the bits they know best. Thus, despite its size, many parts have a definite small town feel to them, each area supporting its own range of shops and other urban facilities. As a visitor you cannot expect to discover much of London during a short stay, so concentrate on getting to know a small part well.

Most visitors and the majority of sensible Londoners travel around London on the underground railway system, which results in something of a rabbit mentality. You will soon find that the city divides itself up into the areas which can be reached from a particular station, and it can be a refreshing discovery that the places which are linked by a coloured line on a tube map are actually connected above ground as well — you could even walk from one station's territory to the next. Never underestimate how long it can take to get from one part of the city to another; they say that city living is efficient because nothing is very far away, but don't believe them.

Regional Tourist Office: London Tourist Board, 26 Grosvenor Gardens, London SW1W 0DU (Tel: 01 730 3450).

Tourist Information Centres: 12 Regent Street (Tel: 01 730 3400); also at Heathrow Airport; Victoria Station; 35 St John's Square, Clerkenwell; Tower of London.

Open Spaces: The decision as to which of the larger open spaces to visit whilst in London may well depend on which area of the city has become your home base. In the north, Hampstead Heath is the ready choice, with its variety of woods and open grassland and the landscaped gardens of Kenwood at the northern end. You can take a brisk walk up Parliament Hill, popular site of kite flyers with a panoramic view of the city; or a stroll past Highgate ponds, where swimming is permitted to the hardy, up to the woods and gardens of Kenwood, returning via the Hampstead Tearooms, surely one of the best in London, for a special treat.

In the east, Greenwich Park provides the largest open space, seeming larger than its 200 acres. The old Royal Observatory, the National Maritime Museum and the Cutty Sark ensure a constant flow of visitors, but there are many hidden corners too, like the deer-inhabited Wilderness in the south-east corner and the traditional gardens of The Dell.

Richmond Park in the south-west is ten times larger than Greenwich and, together with Wimbledon Common, only a dangerous stone's-throw away across the busy A3, provides a piece of what could almost be imagined as open country were it not for the constant roar of traffic. The fallow deer are a feature of Richmond Park, most of which is a rolling savannah-like plain dotted with plantations fenced against the predations of deer and humans.

Altogether there are over 66 square miles of open space in the Greater London area, a much higher proportion than in most Western cities, and with the exception of parts of the East End, Southwark and Lambeth, you are unlikely to be out of walking range of a London park. There are a couple of good guides to London's parks: the best and most expensive is Alec Forshaw and Theo Bergström's *The Open Spaces of London* (Allison and Busby, 1986, £19.95), though Roy Hawkins' *Green London* (Sidgwick and Jackson, 1988, £6.95) is also good.

Wildlife Sites and Nature Reserves: As well as its parks, London has nearly forty important designated wildlife sites, including a couple of dozen national nature reserves. The London Wildlife Trust (80 York Way, London N1 9AG) produces an excellent brief guide called *Wildlife Sites in London* which includes short descriptions and details of how to get there. A few of these sites are worth a particular mention.

Camley Street Natural Park is only a short walk from Kings Cross and St Pancras stations, wedged between the Regents Canal and a gas works. Yet in just two acres you will find a pond, a wildlife garden and a wildflower meadow; dragonflies and damselflies; moorhens and tufted ducks.

On a larger scale, the five acres of the Gunnersbury Triangle (access near Chiswick Park tube station) allow you to wander through birchwood, swamp and oak woodland in the heart of industrial Chiswick, a triumph of conservation over development.

Lavender Pond in Rotherhithe is a good example of an entirely artificial wildlife environment; nearby are Russia Dock Woodlands and Ecological Park and Surrey Docks Urban Farm. On the other side of the river, in Tower Hamlets, St Jude's Nature Park in St Jude's Road is a good example of a small nature garden, much used by local schools but open to all interested and careful visitors.

City Farms: There are over a dozen city farm and city garden projects in the capital. Hackney (Goldsmiths Row), Kentish Town (Cressfield Close) and Vauxhall (Tyers Street) each have a thriving city farm, while Mudchute Farm in Pier Street in London's Docklands is a pioneer farm in several respects. Opened in 1977, much of the farm occupies reclaimed land, and has a very wide range of livestock, including several breeds of horses. Deen City Farm in Mitcham (Batsworth Road, off Church Road; Colliers Wood tube) has a number of experimental organic plots.

Green Walks: If you are prepared to travel out to Epping or Richmond you can walk for several hours without having to tramp the city streets, but there are a few well-planned alternatives. One pleasant and fairly central walk is the 8½ miles of the Regents Canal towpath from the euphemistically-named Little Venice in Paddington to the Thames at Limehouse. The British Waterways Board (Melbury House, Melbury Terrace, London NW1 6JX) has produced several fascinating leaflets about the canal, including one describing canalside wildlife.

In south London, four enlightened boroughs have worked together to create a 15-mile walk called the Green Chain, linking over 300 public and private open spaces. Four leaflets describing the walk can be obtained from Greenwich Planning Department (John Humphries House, Stockwell Street, London SE10 9JN).

In June 1988, the Countryside Commission announced that it was going ahead with plans for a 180-mile-long Thames Path, including a riverside walkway right through central London on both north and south banks as far east as the Thames Barrier. Despite many problems of access and construction, the Thames Path is planned to be complete within twenty years. In the meantime, much of the riverside is already accessible, including long stretches in Kew and Putney as well as the Westminster embankments.

Museums: London is a city of museums, and your whole time could be spent walking round them. If you want to know about London's past and how it has affected the present, however, you can't do much better than visit the Museum of London at London Wall. The Geffrye Museum in Kingsland Road shows what the insides of London houses would have looked like, with period rooms from 1600 to 1939.

Of the many other London museums, here are three small ones which it would be easy to miss; admission to all three is free. The

Museum of Garden History at St-Mary-at-Lambeth in Lambeth Road shows what the English garden would have looked like in the seventeenth century; here too are the graves of the two John Tradescants, father and son, who revolutionised gardening by bringing many of our now-familiar plants back with them from their foreign travels.

The William Morris Gallery in Walthamstow (Water House, Lloyds Park, Forest Row) houses many of the designs of the founder of the 'arts and crafts movement'. Textiles, furniture, ceramics and stained glass are all on display, and you can buy some very tasteful and useful gifts at the little shop.

London's Jewish Museum, upstairs in the Jewish Communal Centre in Upper Woburn Place near Euston station, is not easy to find, but well worth the effort. There is a great deal crammed into a small space, with a very helpful curator if you have any questions.

Building Traditions: London has tens of thousands of listed (historically important) buildings; the best guide is Edward Jones and Christopher Woodward's *Guide to the Architecture of London* (Weidenfeld and Nicolson, 1978, £8.50). There are also around a thousand local amenity societies in the capital, not to mention the headquarters of the important Georgian Group and Victorian Society, each concerned with the conservation of important buildngs from the relevant periods. If you are particularly interested in London's built heritage, a good place to start is the Civic Trust (17 Carlton House Terrace, London SW1Y 5AW); the Trust has a comprehensive library which can be consulted with advance notice.

Transport: It is madness to drive a car in London; especially in the city centre you will almost certainly get to where you want faster by public transport. With 273 stations on nine lines, the Underground is fast and efficient, though not as cheap as it should be. Buy a Travelcard or Capitalcard, which allows you unlimited travel after 9.30 on weekdays or all day at weekends; a 7-day ticket works out even cheaper per journey. London Underground (55 Broadway, London SW1H 0BD) produces a free guide to fares called *Tickets*, and free Underground maps can be obtained from information offices at certain stations.

The Travelcard and Capitalcard also permit travel on London's red buses, which are harder to use than the tube, but often more economical. You will need a *London Bus Map* from information centres or from London Buses (Freepost, Southall UB2 4BR), who can also supply timetables and local bus guides. Many bus stops display timetables and maps of the locality. London buses are easier for visitors to use than is usually imagined; try them and see.

London

London's docklands have recently witnessed two exiting innovations in urban transport — and I'm not referring to the noisy London City Airport. The Docklands Light Railway was opened in 1987, with trains running every ten minutes, giving impressive views over the West India and Millwall Docks. The summer of 1988 saw the launch of the express riverboat service from Charing Cross Pier to the West India Docks. There are plans to extend this frequent and efficient river link westwards to Chelsea and eastwards to Greenwich.

In the last ten years, London has seen a massive rise — 300% — in the number of people regularly cycling around the city. A great deal of the impetus for this increase, and for the environmental improvements that have made it possible, has come from the London Cycling Campaign (Tress House, 3 Stamford Street, London SE1 9NT). There are cycleways in many parts of the city, and the LCC are looking for 1,000 miles of cycle routes in the next ten years. *On Your Bike*, published by the LCC (1986, £1.35) shows cycle routes in London, though is now a little out of date.

The London Tourist Board can provide an up-to-date list of cycle hirers in the city; among the best are On Yer Bike at 52-54 Tooley Street and Porchester Cycles at 8 Porchester Place.

Peace Projects: In Battersea Park you will find one of England's two peace pagodas, erected by the Nipponzan Myohoji Buddhists as part of an international network of visible symbols of peace (the other is in Milton Keynes). Also in the Park is the Sri Chinmoy Peace Mile, a permanent track for runners.

There are peace parks at Maygrove Road in Kilburn and Elthorne Park, Hornsey Rise in Upper Holloway. In Tavistock Square you will find a statue of Mahatma Gandhi and several 'peace trees', while in the Jubilee Gardens alongside County Hall on the South Bank is a monument commemorating women's work for peace.

Every Friday evening there is a peace vigil at Marble Arch, details of which can be obtained at Friends House in Euston Road; there are often such vigils in other places, such as Parliament Square. There is a continuous peace picket at the South African Embassy in Trafalgar Square, which like-minded people are welcome to join.

Community Initiatives:

Community Housing and Architecture: The most visited triumph of community initiative in London is Covent Garden, which but for the tireless dedication of a handful of its residents might today consist of yet more anonymous office blocks. Since 1971 the local community association has overseen the building of housing, a community-run recreation centre, shops and restaurants, retaining

London

the area's traditional mixture of uses. Look out particularly for the new Jubilee Hall in Southampton Street and the trompe l'oeil mural on the corner of Russell Street.

For an example of what can be done with an unprepossessing high-rise block when it comes to 'redevelopment', visit Lea View House, off Clapton Common in North Hackney. In 1982 the residents of this five-storey 300 flat estates took matters into their own hands, and working with the local authority's direct labour organisation and architects came up with a scheme which provided what the residents actually needed. Compared with many high-rise schemes, Lea View is clean and attractive, its residents having proved that community involvement works.

At Brockley Park in Lewisham you can see self-help housing on a different scale. In Segal Close the self-build housing techniques pioneered by architect Walter Segal have been used to build a prototype street of 'home-made' houses; at number 6 you will find the Segal Trust, willing to tell you all about their work in promoting self-built houses.

At Coin Street, just behind the National Theatre on the South Bank, low-cost housing association homes have been built for 300 people, thus meeting the real needs of Londoners in an area where commercially-built houses cost upwards of a quarter of a million.

There are of course many other interesting projects you could visit; if you tell them exactly what you want, ACTAC (see page 46) should be able to supply details.

Other Community Activities: In terms of organised community activities, the London boroughs are generally both generous and imaginative. From sponsored bike rides to children's picnics, street festivals to open-air theatre, you can usually find something stimulating to involve yourself in. One imaginative community-based project is the Rio Community Cinema in Kingsland High Street, where local people have not only reopened the cinema itself but have also provided meeting rooms and a community exhibiton space; call in for a programme. Libraries are a good place to ask for information about local activities, and most boroughs have an information centre too.

Communal Groups: There are several long-established communal groups in London, though they are mostly on the small side and have a fairly rapid turnover of residents; most do not have accommodation for travellers, though do welcome interested visitors. I won't give addresses here since I wouldn't wish them to be mobbed by *Green Guide* readers, though if you leaf through the *Communes Network Directory* (see page 50) and ring ahead, you will almost certainly be welcome to share a cup of tea and a chat.

London

Economic Initiatives

Co-operatives: There are getting on for 500 co-ops in Greater London; the Greater London CDA (80 Waynflete Street, W10) will be able to help with specific enquiries. One place where the co-operative movement has had very tangible results is in Hackney, where Bradbury Street is in effect a street of co-ops, including a bicycle shop, Matrix feminist architects, an African drum manufacturers and a video co-op. On Saturdays there is a market in the street, so you can buy the produce of many of the local companies. Many of the enterprises mentioned under other headings are co-ops, and of those not otherwise mentioned, you might like to visit Earth Exchange wholefood and bookshop at 213 Archway Road, Highgate; Mother Africa Records at 177 Upper Street, Islington; or England's largest recycled paper company, Paperback, at 8-16 Coronet Street, Hoxton.

Craft Workshops: The London Tourist Board produces a useful and free *Guide to Markets* in the city, which will tell you where to go for what. For crafts the best places are The Courtyard alongside St-Martin-in-the-Fields, the Jubilee Hall in Covent Garden (Saturday and Sunday), the Piccadilly Market in front of St James's Church (Friday and Saturday), and Brixton Market on a Saturday. The Crafts Council at 12 Waterloo Place is a good source of information, while the British Crafts Centre at 43 Earlham Street often has good displays. Worth visiting too is the Craftsmen Potters' Shop at William Blake House, 7 Marshall Street, but the prices can be breathtaking.

Energy Initiatives

Nuclear and Anti-Nuclear: There are no nuclear power stations in the Greater London area, though the London Nuclear Information Unit (141 Euston Road, NW1) has identified over 90 locations in the city relating to what they call 'the nuclear maze'. Their free publication, *Nuclear London*, is obtainable from them, as is an investigation, entitled *The Nuclear Trains*, of the transport of nuclear waste through the city.

Alternative Energy: London today has no working watermills and only one working windmill, in Blenheim Gardens behind Brixton Prison, though there is a windmill museum in Wimbledon, appropriately enough in Windmill Road.

On the other hand, there have been several successful schemes to incorporate solar heating systems into both new and existing buildings. NATTA (see page 45) have produced a guide to *Solar Houses in London* (1985, £1), and among the projects you can view are 14 rehabilitated Victorian houses in Whateley Road, East

London

Dulwich and 18 new energy-efficient houses in Lawrie Park Road, Sydenham.

In recent years there has been an emphasis on energy efficiency, and much talk of local combined-heat-and-power schemes. There is little as yet to see on the ground, though it is possible with advance notice to visit the Edmonton incinerator, to the north of the city, which burns a tenth of the capital's garbage and sells electricity to the national grid.

Health: Practitioners of almost every therapy known to humankind can be found somewhere in London. The Institute for Complementary Medicine at 21 Portland Place operates a referral service, and prefers to deal with personal callers. Of the many natural health centres in the city, the Community Health Foundation at 188 Old Street (Tel: 01-251 4076) and Isis at 362 High Road, Tottenham (Tel: 01-808 6401) stand out, both covering a wide range of treatments.

Food: There are so many restaurants in London that finding good and wholesome fare, especially in the more central areas, is not usually a problem. It is well worth investing in a copy of Sarah Brown's slim volume *Vegetarian London* (Thorsons, 1988, £3.50), which describes more than a hundred places offering decent vegetarian food (many of them are not 100% vegetarian, but all are oriented towards a healthy diet). Places which are worth going out of your way to visit include Food for Thought at 31 Neal Street; Raw Deal at 65 Paddington Street; and the Greenhouse at 16 Chenies Street. You will find branches of the famous Cranks throughout the West End, their main restaurant at 8 Marshall Street offering a 'wine and dine' evening to remember at around £10 a head. The London Ecology Centre at 45 Shelton Street offers light meals in a convenient location, as does the Neal's Yard tea room.

There are also several excellent Indian restaurants serving tasty vegetarian food (try the Diwana at 121 Drummond Street, near Euston station, or the Raj Bhelpoori at 19 Camden High Street); The Olive Tree at 11 Wardour Street offers excellent value-for-money Middle Eastern fare.

Bookshops: In Charing Cross Road, a time-honoured location for bookshops, you will find Books for a Change (green issues, Third World, peace, plus recycled stationery) at number 52, with Silver Moon women's bookshop at number 68. London's other women's bookshop is Sisterwrite at 190 Upper Street, Islington, with a women's gallery upstairs. Gay's The Word, the country's leading gay and lesbian bookshop, is at 66 Marchmont Street, Bloomsbury.

Every appropriate technology text you could ever want will be found at the Intermediate Technology Bookshop at 103-105 Southampton Row, not far from Russell Square tube, while the

London Ecology Centre at 45 Shelton Street sells a limited range of 'green' books. For books on Third World and development issues, Third World Publications have a shop in the Africa Centre at 38 King Street, while Soma Books at 38 Kennington Lane carries a wide range of Third World books and crafts.

The specialist bookseller for books on alternative health is Robert Chris at 8 Cecil Court, off Charing Cross Road, while opposite at 19 and 21 Cecil Court is London's best-known 'esoteric' bookshop, Watkins. For therapy, the place to go is Changes Bookshop at 242 Belsize Road, Belsize Park.

Housmans at 5 Caledonia Road, just round the corner from Kings Cross station, is *the* place for books on peace and related issues, while CND at 22-24 Underwood Street (off City Road) and the bookshop at Friends House, Euston Road also have a smaller range of similar titles.

Central Books at 37 Gray's Inn Road and Collets at 64-66 Charing Cross Road are the bookshops for socialist and communist books, while the friendly Freedom Bookshop in Angel Alley off Whitechapel High Street covers anarchism and radical politics.

For community-based bookshops and information centres, Sunpower at 198 Blackstock Road, Finsbury Park and Centreprise at 136-138 Kingsland High Street, Hackney, are both worth a visit. For the best range of books covering all of the above interests, however, you can't do much better than spend a couple of hours browsing the shelves of Compendium at 234 Camden High Street, a large, airy and friendly shop near Camden Lock.

Local Resources: *City Limits* (a weekly what's-on guide produced by a worker's co-operative) will provide up-to-date information about events in the capital city, together with in-depth articles and a fascinating lonely hearts column.

The London Ecology Centre is a good place to pick up literature about green happenings, while Friends of the Earth's main office at 26-28 Underwood Street (near Old Street tube) can usually provide more detailed information. There are rumours of a new edition of the classic *Alternative London* being in the offing, and tentative plans for a Londonwide green directory. Look out for them.

Time Out, *City Limits*'s rival on the what's on scene, produces a very useful *Shopping in London* guide at £3.50, while of the very many London guidebooks now available I will mention a handful that I particularly like. David Brazil's *Naked City: 150 Faces of Hidden London* (Macdonald, 1987, £4.95) is a guide to the city's lesser-known but nonetheless fascinating landmarks. *The Absolutely Essential Guide to London* (Sphere, 1986, £4.95) is David Benedictus's idiosyncratic but highly readable choice of all the best and worst that London has to offer. In *The Pink Plaque Guide to*

London (GMP, 1986, £5.95) Michael Elliman and Frederick Roll trace the London lives of over a hundred celebrated gay men and women, while Jennifer Clarke has written a similar and just as fascinating guide based on the lives of 270 famous women, *In Our Grandmothers' Footsteps* (Virago, 1984, £4.95).

Changes and corrections, August 1989

page 76 (Durham):
Earthcare are in fact much more than just a craft shop, stocking a wide range of 'environment-friendly' products and a good selection of green books. For Third World crafts in Durham, visit Gateway Crafts in St Nicholas' Church, Market Place.

page 119 (The Shires):
The Rural Life Museum at Stoke Bruerne has now closed.

page 131 (East Anglia):
Norfolk Lavender point out that though they do not use pesticides and do use organic fertilisers, they also use a mild herbicide to control couch grass, and so are not strictly organic — would that all growers were so honest!

page 137 (Bristol):
Bristol's Tourist Information Office is now at 14 Narrow Quay (Tel: 0272 260767.
Full Marks bookshop has now closed.

page 141 (Glastonbury):
Bicycles may now be hired from Pedallers, 8 Magdalene Street.

Do please keep sending us your corrections and updates!

GREEN GUIDE TO ENGLAND UPDATE FORM

To: The Green Guide to England,
Green Print, The Merlin Press Ltd,
10 Malden Road, London NW5 3HR.

From: Name:

Address:

For inclusion in future editions of *The Green Guide to England*, I would like to draw the compiler's attention to the following:

....

GREEN GUIDE TO ENGLAND UPDATE FORM

To: The Green Guide to England,
Green Print, The Merlin Press Ltd,
10 Malden Road, London NW5 3HR.

From: Name:

Address:

For inclusion in future editions of *The Green Guide to England*, I would like to draw the compiler's attention to the following: